The media's watch

Here's a sampling of our coverage.

> the most trusted name in career information™

VAULT CAREER GUIDE TO
INVESTMENT
BANKING

VAULT CAREER GUIDE TO
INVESTMENT BANKING

TOM LOTT, DEREK LOOSVELT, WILLIAM JARVIS
AND THE STAFF OF VAULT

Library of Congress CIP Data is available.

ISBN 10 : 1-58131-532-5

ISBN 13 : 978-1-58131-532-5

Printed in the United States of America

ACKNOWLEDGMENTS

We are extremely grateful to Vault's entire staff for all their help in the editorial, production and marketing processes. Vault also would like to acknowledge the support of our investors, clients, employees, family, and friends. Thank you!

Are you ready to bring your **determination** to the world's economy?

At Lehman Brothers, your passion, drive and commitment can make an impact from day one.

Whether you are interested in a career in investment banking, capital markets, investment management or any of our corporate areas, visit us online at www.lehman.com/ruready.

lehman.com/ruready

LEHMAN BROTHERS

Table of Contents

THE INDUSTRY

Chapter 7: M&A, Private Placements, and Reorgs   61

ON THE JOB

Chapter 8: Corporate Finance   73

Chapter 9: Institutional Sales and Trading   103

Chapter 10: Research   139

Visit the Vault Finance Career Channel at **www.vault.com/finance** – with
insider firm profiles, message boards, the Vault Finance Job Board and more.

VAULT CAREER LIBRARY

xi

Chapter 11: Syndicate: The Go-Betweens   155

APPENDIX

GO FOR THE GOLD!

THE INDUSTRY

What is Investment Banking?

CHAPTER 1

What is investment banking? Is it investing? Is it banking? Really, it is neither. Investment banking, or I-banking, as it is often called, is the term used to describe the business of raising capital for companies and advising them on financing and merger alternatives. Capital essentially means money. Companies need cash in order to grow and expand their businesses; investment banks sell securities (debt and equity) to investors in order to raise this cash. These securities can come in the form of stocks, bonds, or loans, which we will discuss in depth later. Once issued, these securities trade in the global financial markets.

The Players

The biggest investment banks include Goldman Sachs, JPMorgan, Merrill Lynch, Morgan Stanley, Credit Suisse, Citigroup's Global Corporate Investment Bank, and Lehman Brothers, among others. Of course, the complete list of I-banks is substantially more extensive, but the firms listed above compete for the biggest deals both in the U.S. and worldwide. They are usually referred to as "bulge bracket" investment banks.

You have probably heard of many of these firms, and perhaps have a brokerage account with the commercial banking arm of one of them. While the brokerage presence of these firms covers every major city in the U.S., the headquarters of almost every one of these firms is in New York City, the epicenter of the I-banking universe. It is important to realize that investment banking and brokerage go hand-in-hand, but that brokers are one small cog in the investment banking wheel. As we will cover in detail later, brokers sell securities and manage the portfolios of "retail" (or individual) investors.

This raises a very important distinction in the world of investment banking. A number of firms have remained "pure" investment banks (Goldman Sachs, Lehman Brothers, Morgan Stanley), while others have commercial banking arms (JPMorgan, Citigroup, Bank of America). Until recently, these two were completely separate entities; while the investment bank would provide M&A and other strategic financial advice to companies, the commercial bank would lend capital (often times the advice requires capital). However, as firms evolved, many found they could become "one

Visit the Vault Finance Career Channel at www.vault.com/finance – with insider firm profiles, message boards, the Vault Finance Job Board and more.

VAULT CAREER LIBRARY

3

stop shopping" for M&A advice, bond offerings, etc. for clients. These global financial institutions are able to tap the vast network of deep relationships they have with small clients and turn those into large transactions as the clients become larger. As you will see from the league tables (discussed later), many of these investment banks with commercial arms are the biggest dealmakers on Wall Street.

Many an I-banking interviewee asks, "Which firm is the best?" The answer, like many things in life, is unclear. There are many ways to measure the quality of investment banks. You might examine a bank's expertise in a certain segment of investment banking. For example, Citigroup was tops in 2006 in total debt and equity underwriting volume, but trailed Goldman Sachs in mergers and acquisitions ("M&A") advisory. Goldman Sachs, as a pure investment bank, has a stellar reputation in equity underwriting and M&A advisory but is not nearly as strong in debt issuance.

The debt markets belong to the larger investment banks with commercial banking arms, such as Citigroup and JPMorgan. With larger balance sheets (due to customer deposits, among a variety of other things), these banks are able to leverage their size to take on more underwriting risk (more on underwriting later). By underwriting more transactions and becoming a one-stop-shop, these firms now have a very substantial presence in M&A, IPO, and equity-related volume. They can focus on executing every possible deal in the market, whereas the pure investment banks might focus on a particular area (M&A at Goldman, for example).

Those who watch the industry pay attention to "league tables," which are rankings of investment banks in several categories (e.g., equity underwriting or M&A advisory). The most commonly referred to league tables are published quarterly by Thomson

Financial Securities Data (TFSD), a research firm based in Newark, N.J. TFSD collects data on deals done in a given time period and determines which firm has done the most deals in a given sector over that time period. Essentially, the league tables are rankings of firm by quantity of deals in a given area.

However, readers should be aware that the only truly unbiased source of information comes from these independent firms, such as Thomson, and not from the investment banks themselves. League tables are merely a compilation of the volume of transactions (either by deal size or by number of deals) and can be easily manipulated by the investment banks for bragging purposes. For example, in just about every pitch made to a client, there will usually be a page with tombstones (icons of previous deals done by an I-bank), along with league tables, showing the firm's expertise in a given area. Many times, analysts and associates will find themselves creating favorable league tables at late hours of the night to show how their firm is truly the best in a particular market segment, for transactions of a certain size, and so forth.

Vault also provides prestige rankings of the Top 50 banking firms, based on surveys of finance professionals. These rankings are available on our web site, www.vault.com.

Of course, industry rankings and prestige ratings don't tell a firm's whole story. Since the pay scale in the industry tends to be comparable among different firms, potential investment bankers would be wise to pay attention to the quality of life at the firms they're considering for employment. This includes culture, social life and hours, which differs greatly even within different groups at the same firm. You can glean this information from your job interviews as well as reports on the firms available from Vault.

Visit the Vault Finance Career Channel at **www.vault.com/finance** – with insider firm profiles, message boards, the Vault Finance Job Board and more.

VAULT CAREER LIBRARY

5

The Game

Generally, the breakdown of an investment bank includes the following areas:

Corporate Finance (equity)
Corporate Finance (debt)
Mergers & Acquisitions (M&A)
Equity Capital Markets
Debt Capital Markets
Equity Sales
Fixed Income Sales
Syndicate (equity)
Syndicate (debt)
Equity Trading
Fixed Income Trading
Equity Research
Fixed Income Research

The functions of all of these areas will be discussed in much more detail later in the book. In this overview section, we will cover the nuts and bolts of the business, providing an overview of the stock and bond markets and how an I-bank operates within them.

Corporate finance

The bread and butter of a traditional investment bank, corporate finance generally performs two different functions: 1) Mergers and acquisitions advisory and 2) Underwriting.

(1) **On the mergers and acquisitions (M&A)** advising side of corporate finance, bankers assist in negotiating and structuring mergers between companies. If, for example, a company wants to buy another firm, then an investment bank will help finalize the purchase price, structure the deal, and generally ensure a smooth transaction. In the last few years, the M&A market has been white-hot, as companies have large cash balances with which they can complete strategic transactions.

(2) **The underwriting function** within corporate finance involves the process of raising capital for a company. In the investment banking

world, capital can be raised by selling either equity (stocks) or debt (bonds or loans) (as well as some more exotic securities) to investors. Underwriting is unique, in that it involves the investment bank assuming a large amount of risk. Essentially, in the case of a bond offering, you can think of the process of underwriting as an investment bank writing a check to a company, then raising the funds in the markets from investors. This means that the investment bank assumes the risk of the transaction not selling in the market. Think of this as buying pizza for friends and relying on them to pay you back. If you've ever done this, you've "underwritten" a transaction.

Although performing two functions, corporate finance is often divided into a number of industry-focused groups, called "coverage" groups. Coverage groups are usually aligned by a client's industry and can potentially include aerospace & defense, automotive, consumer goods, diversified industrials, FIG (financial institutions and governments), financial sponsors, healthcare, natural resources (oil & gas, metals & mining, power), TMT (technology, media, telecom), real estate, and transportation. As these groups focus on industries and relationships, they are able to become very close to the clients and their needs. Therefore, it is not uncommon for M&A advisory work to either be done within these groups, or as a completely separate group, also broken into industry coverage teams.

As those in corporate finance are privy to private company information, such as forward-looking financials, they are considered on the "private side" of the so-called Chinese wall and are unable to sell or trade such privileged information.

Capital markets

The role of capital markets is managing the interaction of the bankers in corporate finance with those in sales & trading (as well as research). Generally placed under the "corporate finance" umbrella, these jobs blend a bit of both corporate finance and sales & trading. Capital markets professionals are responsible for understanding recent transactions in the financial markets and using this information to structure new transactions. They serve as invaluable market advisors for their firm's deals and many times are the leads in executing deals originated from other areas in corporate finance. Capital markets professionals are also usually grouped into either equity capital markets or debt capital markets.

As they are also privy to private information, such as forward-looking financials of companies, capital markets personnel are also on the "private side" of the Chinese wall.

Visit the Vault Finance Career Channel at **www.vault.com/finance** – with insider firm profiles, message boards, the Vault Finance Job Board and more.

VAULT CAREER LIBRARY

7

Sales

Sales is another core component of any investment bank. Salespeople take the form of: 1) the classic retail broker, 2) the institutional salesperson, or 3) the private client service representative. Retail brokers develop relationships with individual investors and sell stocks and stock advice to the average Joe. Institutional salespeople develop business relationships with large institutional investors. Institutional investors are those who manage large groups of assets, for example pension funds, mutual funds, hedge funds, or large corporations. Private Client Service (PCS) representatives are somewhere between retail brokers and institutional salespeople in the spectrum, providing brokerage and money management services for extremely wealthy individuals. Salespeople make money through commissions on trades made through their firms or, increasingly, as a percentage of their clients' assets with the firm.

As investment bankers structure transactions requiring the issuance of new securities, salespeople are responsible for selling these securities to investors. Therefore, although a transaction might appear profitable on paper, it ultimately relies on those buying the securities and the investment bank's relationships with those buyers. Furthermore, as those securities trade in the market, the salespeople are responsible for representing their clients and executing a purchase or sale on their behalf.

As they usually interact with the public financial markets and do not have private information, sales people are generally considered to be on the public side of the Chinese wall.

Trading

Traders provide a vital role for the investment bank. In general, traders facilitate the buying and selling of stocks, bonds, and other securities such as currencies, futures, and derivatives, either by carrying an inventory of securities for sale or by executing a given trade for a client.

A trader plays two distinct roles for an investment bank:

(1) **Providing liquidity:** Traders provide liquidity to the firm's clients (that is, providing clients with the ability to buy or sell a security on demand). Traders do this by standing ready to buy the client's securities at any time (or sell securities to the client) if the client needs to place a trade quickly. This is also called making a market, or acting as a market maker. Traders performing this function make money for the firm by selling securities at a slightly higher price than they pay for them. This price differential is known as the bid-ask spread. (The bid price at any

given time is the price at which an investor can sell a security to another, which is usually slightly lower than the ask price, which is the price at which investors can buy the same security from another investor.)

(2) Proprietary trading: In addition to providing liquidity and executing traders for the firm's customers, traders also may take their own trading positions on behalf of the firm, using the firm's capital hoping to benefit from the rise or fall in the price of securities. This is called proprietary trading. Typically, the marketing-making function and the proprietary trading function is performed by the same trader for any given security. For example, Morgan Stanley's Five Year Treasury Note trader will typically both make a market in the 5-Year Note as well as take trading positions in the 5-Year Note for Morgan Stanley's own account.

Furthermore, a number of investment banks have standalone proprietary trading operations, whereby they act like independent hedge funds, investing the firm's capital in an effort to maximize returns. Of the major investment banks, JPMorgan has the largest hedge fund presence with over $34 billion in assets under management, followed closely by Goldman Sachs. This hedge-fund style investing is prevalent at most all investment banks, but has come under much scrutiny at Goldman Sachs, where the firm's revenues and pre-tax income from 2006 were substantially concentrated in "principal investing." According to the firm's annual report, close to 70 percent of its revenues and pre-tax income were concentrated in this investing area.

As traders make markets and take positions in securities, they are considered on the public side of the Chinese wall. Unlike corporate finance investment bankers, they are not allowed private information, due to SEC regulations.

Research

Research analysts follow stocks and bonds and make recommendations to outside investors on whether to buy, sell, or hold those securities. They also forecast companies' future earnings. Stock analysts (known as equity analysts) typically focus on one industry and will cover up to 20 companies' stocks at any given time. Some research analysts work on the fixed income side and will cover a particular segment, such as a particular industry's high yield bonds. Salespeople within the I-bank utilize research published by analysts to convince their clients to buy or sell securities through their firm. Corporate finance bankers rely on research analysts to be experts in the industry in which they are working. Reputable research analysts can generate substantial corporate finance business for their firm as well as

Visit the Vault Finance Career Channel at **www.vault.com/finance** — with
insider firm profiles, message boards, the Vault Finance Job Board and more.

VAULT CAREER LIBRARY

9

substantial trading activity, and thus are an integral part of any investment bank.

Research areas are usually placed under the sales & trading umbrella, due to the nature of their work in the financial markets. They too are part of the public side of the Chinese wall, using only public information to construct financial models and make recommendations. In some cases, successful research analysts will be recruited to work for the proprietary trading operations of an investment bank or will even be recruited by top-tier hedge funds due to their depth of knowledge of certain securities and markets.

Syndicate

The hub of the investment banking wheel, the syndicate group provides a vital link between salespeople and corporate finance. Syndicate exists to facilitate the placing of securities in a public offering, a knock-down drag-out affair between and among buyers of offerings and the investment banks managing the process. In a corporate or municipal debt deal, syndicate also determines the allocation of bonds and loans. As the function is the hub of the wheel, it often works very closely with the professionals in capital markets.

Syndicate is also occasionally referred to as "primary sales," where securities are placed into the hands of investors for the first time. Once allocated to an investor, any trading of these securities happens in the secondary markets, which are what most people think of when they think of the financial markets. However, to avoid confusion, the primary markets are usually just referred to as "syndicate."

Commercial Banking, Investment Banking and Asset Management

Before describing how an investment bank operates, let's back up and start by describing traditional commercial banking. Commercial and investment banking share many aspects, but also have many fundamental differences. After a quick overview of commercial banking, we will build up to a full discussion of what I-banking entails.

Although the barriers between investment and commercial banks have essentially been removed by the passage of the Gramm-Leach-Bliley Financial Services Modernization Act of 1999, we will for now examine the traditional model of the commercial banking industry and compare it to investment banking. We will then investigate how the new legislation affects commercial and investment banking organizations. Also, we will distinguish between the "buy-side" and the "sell-side" of the securities industry.

It's important to note that a number of banks have both commercial and investment banking operations. The largest and most active of these include JPMorganChase, Citigroup, and Bank of America. All three have separate entities for each function: commercial banking and investment banking. The synergy gained from their presence in both areas has enabled them to grow at astounding rates.

Commercial Banking vs. Investment Banking

While regulation has changed the businesses in which commercial and investment banks may now participate, the core aspects of these different businesses remain intact. In other words, the difference between how a typical investment bank and a typical commercial operate bank can be simplified: A commercial bank takes deposits for checking and savings accounts from consumers, while an investment bank does not. We'll begin examining what this means by taking a look at what commercial banks do.

Commercial banks

A commercial bank may legally take deposits for checking and savings accounts from consumers. The federal government provides insurance guarantees on these deposits through the Federal Deposit Insurance Corporation (the FDIC), on amounts up to $100,000. To get FDIC guarantees, commercial banks must follow a myriad of regulations.

The typical commercial banking process is fairly straightforward. You deposit money into your bank, and the bank loans that money to consumers and companies in need of capital (cash). You borrow to buy a house,

finance a car, or finance an addition to your home. Companies borrow to finance the growth of their company or meet immediate cash needs. Companies that borrow from commercial banks range in size from the local dry cleaner to the multinational conglomerate such as GE, IBM, and Exxon Mobil. The commercial bank generates a profit by paying depositors a lower interest rate than the bank charges on loans. Examples of commercial banks include Chase, Bank of America, Citibank, PNC, and Wachovia.

Private contracts

Importantly, loans from commercial banks to individuals are structured as private legally binding contracts between two parties—the bank and you (or the bank and a company). Banks work with their clients to individually determine the terms of the loans, including the time to maturity and the interest rate charged. Your individual credit history (or credit risk profile) determines the amount you can borrow and how much interest you are charged. Perhaps you need to borrow $200,000 to purchase a home, or maybe you need $30,000 to finance the purchase of a car. Maybe for the first loan, you and the bank will agree that you pay an interest rate of 7.5 percent; perhaps for the car loan, the interest rate will be 6 percent. The rates are determined through a negotiation between you and the bank.

Let's take another minute to understand how a bank makes its money. On most loans, commercial banks in the U.S. earn interest anywhere from five to 14 percent. Ask yourself how much your bank pays you on your deposits—the money that it uses to make loans. You probably earn a paltry one percent on a checking account, if anything, and maybe three to four percent on a savings account. Commercial banks thus make money by taking advantage of the large spread between their cost of funds (one percent, for example) and their return on funds loaned (ranging from five to 14 percent).

Commercial banks also make a substantial portion of their revenues from lending to corporations of all sizes. As companies seek to expand operations, they might use a loan to purchase a fleet of cars, or land to build a new headquarters. These loans are structured just like those to individuals, with an interest rate based on the credit worthiness of the company. Even the largest and most stable of companies, General Electric, has loans from commercial banks. However, as loans to large corporations are usually much larger in size (GE's credit lines are estimated to be over $25 billion), commercial banks tend to divide up the exposure and build a "syndicate" of lenders. Many large commercial loans are even traded by institutional investors in the syndicated loan market.

Investment banks

An investment bank operates quite differently from a commercial bank. An investment bank does not have an inventory of cash deposits to lend as a commercial bank does. In essence, from a market-making perspective, an investment bank acts as an intermediary, and matches sellers of stocks and bonds with buyers of stocks and bonds. An investment bank also provides advisory services (M&A), which does not require it to deal in the securities of the underlying companies.

Note, however, that companies use investment banks toward the same end as they use commercial banks. If a company needs capital, it can raise funds via a loan from a commercial bank or it may also ask an investment bank to sell equity or debt (stocks or bonds) on its behalf in the public markets. Because commercial banks already have funds available from their depositors and an investment bank typically does not, an I-bank must spend considerable time finding investors in order to obtain capital for its client. This is where the investment banks with commercial banking arms excel. Many of these firms have access to billions of dollars of their own capital that they are able to lend immediately to clients in the form of underwriting.

Loans (Private Debt) vs. Bonds (Public Debt) — An Example

Let's look at an example to illustrate the difference between loans and bonds. Suppose Acme Cleaning Company needs capital, and estimates its need to be $50 million. Acme could obtain a commercial bank loan from Bank of New York for the entire $50 million, and pay interest on that loan just like you would pay on a $5,000 personal finance loan from Bank of New York. Alternately, it could sell bonds publicly using an investment bank such as Merrill Lynch. The $50 million bond issue raised by Merrill would be broken into many smaller bonds and then sold to the public. (For example, the issue could be broken into 50,000 bonds, each worth $1,000.) Once sold, the company receives its $50 million (less Merrill's fees) and investors receive bonds worth a total of the same amount.

Over time, the investors in the bond offering receive coupon payments (the interest), and ultimately the principal (the original $1,000) at the end of the life of the loan, when Acme Corp buys back the bonds (retires the bonds). Thus, we see that in a bond offering, while the money is still loaned to Acme, it is actually loaned by numerous investors, rather than from a single bank.

Because the investment bank involved in the offering does not own the bonds but merely placed them with investors at the outset, it earns no interest—the bondholders earn this interest in the form of regular coupon payments. The investment bank makes money by charging the client (in this case, Acme) a small percentage of the transaction upon its completion, while not holding the bonds. Investment banks call this upfront fee the "underwriting discount." In contrast, a commercial bank making a loan of $50MM actually receives the interest and simultaneously owns the debt, or a portion thereof.

Traditionally, for loans less than $50MM, it is typical for a commercial bank to be the sole lender. However, as investors have become more savvy and commercial loans have grown in size, the two markets are now quite similar. For loans larger than $100MM, it is not uncommon for there to be multiple commercial banks organized by an "arranger." In many cases, the loans are large enough and liquid enough to be traded much like bonds in the secondary markets by institutional investors. In fact, the loan and bond markets are so similar that the major distinction is that the loan market is still a private market, whereas the bond market is not (also, the loan instrument is typically a floating-rate instrument, whereas bonds are usually thought of as fixed rate instruments). Thus, commercial banks are receiving the loan's underwriting or arrangement fee (the difference is discussed later in Chapter 4), while also receiving interest on whatever portion of the loan it owns.

Later, we will cover the steps involved in underwriting a public bond deal and a private loan deal. Legally, most bonds must first be approved by the Securities and Exchange Commission (SEC). (The SEC is a government entity that regulates the sale of all public securities.) The investment bankers guide the company through the SEC approval process, and then market the offering utilizing a written prospectus, its sales force and a roadshow to find investors.

The question of equity or debt

Investment banks underwrite stock offerings just as they do bond or loan offerings. In the stock offering process, a company sells a portion of the equity (or ownership) of itself to the investing public. The very first time a company chooses to sell equity, this offering of equity is transacted through a process called an initial public offering of stock (commonly known as an IPO). Through the IPO process, stock in a company is created and sold to the public. After the deal, stock sold in the U.S. is traded on a stock exchange such as the New York Stock Exchange (NYSE) or the NASDAQ. We will cover the equity offering process in greater detail in Chapter 6. The equity underwriting process is another major way in which investment banking differs from commercial banking.

Commercial banks (even before Glass-Steagall repeal) were able to legally underwrite debt, and some of the largest commercial banks have developed substantial expertise in underwriting bond and loan deals. So, not only do these banks make loans utilizing their deposits, they also underwrite deals through a corporate finance department. When it comes to underwriting these debt offerings, commercial banks have long competed for this business directly with investment banks. However, as a practical matter, only the biggest tier of commercial banks are able to do so, because the size of most debt issues is large and Wall Street competition for such deals is quite fierce. Not surprisingly, many of these commercial and investment banking competitors have merged to take advantage of their vast synergies.

Ultimately, when choosing to raise capital, a company might have the option of equity or debt. Debt, representing a repayment obligation, comes with its own set of restrictions, but is usually less expensive than offering equity. However, unlike debt, equity does not require the company to pay regular interest payments to investors, yet it does require the company to sell a portion of itself to the general public. For a variety of reasons, a company might choose to issue one versus the other.

Glass-Steagall Reform

Previously, we briefly discussed that much has recently changed in the investment banking industry, driven primarily by the breakdown of the Glass-Steagall Act. This section will cover why the Act was originally put into place, why it was criticized, and how recent legislation will continue to impact the securities industry.

The history of Glass-Steagall

The famous Glass-Steagall Act, enacted in 1934, erected barriers between commercial banking and the securities industry. A piece of Depression-Era legislation, Glass-Steagall was created in the aftermath of the stock market crash of 1929 and the subsequent collapse of many commercial banks. At the time, many blamed the securities activities of commercial banks for their instability. Dealings in securities, critics claimed, upset the soundness of the banking community, caused banks to fail, and crippled the economy. Therefore, separating securities businesses and commercial banking seemed the best solution to provide solidity to the U.S. banking and securities' system.

In later years, a different truth seemed evident. The framers of Glass-Steagall argued that a conflict of interest existed between commercial and investment banks. The conflict of interest argument ran something like this: 1) A bank that made a bad loan to a corporation might try to reduce its risk of the company defaulting by underwriting a public offering and selling stock in that company; 2) The proceeds from the IPO would be used to pay off the bad loan; and 3) Essentially, the bank would shift risk from its own balance sheet to new investors via the initial public offering. Academic research and common sense, however, has convinced many that this conflict of interest isn't valid. A bank that consistently sells ill-fated stock would quickly lose its reputation and ability to sell IPOs to new investors.

Glass-Steagall's fall in the late 1990s

In the late 1990s, before legislation officially eradicated the Glass-Steagall Act's restrictions, the investment and commercial banking industries witnessed an abundance of commercial banking firms making forays into the I-banking world. The feeding frenzy reached a height in the spring of 1998. In 1998, NationsBank bought Montgomery Securities, Société Génerale bought Cowen & Co., First Union bought Wheat First and Bowles

Hollowell Connor, Bank of America bought Robertson Stephens (and then sold it to BankBoston), Deutsche Bank bought Bankers Trust (which had bought Alex. Brown months before), and Citigroup was created in a merger of Travelers Insurance and Citibank. While some commercial banks have chosen to add I-banking capabilities through acquisitions, some have tried to build their own investment banking business. JPMorgan stands as the best example of a commercial bank that entered the I-banking world through internal growth, although it recently joined forces with Chase Manhattan and, more recently, BankOne to form JPMorganChase. Interestingly, JPMorgan actually used to be both a securities firm and a commercial bank until federal regulators forced the company to separate the divisions. The split resulted in JPMorgan, the commercial bank, and Morgan Stanley, the investment bank. Today, JPMorgan has slowly and steadily clawed its way back to the pinnacle of the securities business, and Morgan Stanley has merged with Dean Witter to create one of the larger I-banks on the Street.

What took so long?

So why did it take so long to enact a repeal of Glass-Steagall? There were several logistical and political issues to address in undoing Glass-Steagall. For example, the FDIC and the Federal Reserve regulate commercial banks, while the SEC regulates securities firms. A debate emerged as to who would regulate the new "universal" financial services firms. The Fed eventually won with Fed Chairman Alan Greenspan defining his office's role as that of an "umbrella supervisor." A second stalling factor involved the Community Reinvestment Act of 1977—an act that requires commercial banks to re-invest a portion of their earnings back into their community. Senator Phil Gramm (R-TX), Chairman of the Senate Banking Committee, was a strong opponent of this legislation while then-President Clinton was in favor of keeping and even expanding CRA. The two sides agreed on a compromise in which CRA requirements were lessened for small banks.

In November 1999, Clinton signed the Gramm-Leach Bliley Act, which repealed restrictions contained in Glass-Steagall that prevent banks from affiliating with securities firms. The new law allows banks, securities firms, and insurance companies to affiliate within a financial holding company ("FHC") structure. Under the new system, insurance, banking, and securities activities are "functionally regulated."

The Buy-Side vs. the Sell-Side

The traditional investment banking world is considered the "sell-side" of the securities industry. Why? Investment banks create stocks and bonds, and sell these securities to investors. Sell is the key word, as I-banks continually sell their firms' capabilities to generate corporate finance business, and salespeople sell securities to generate commission revenue.

Who are the buyers ("buy-side") of public stocks and bonds? They are individual investors (you and me) and institutional investors, firms like Fidelity and Vanguard, and organizations like Harvard University. The universe of institutional investors is appropriately called the buy-side of the securities industry and includes asset managers, pension funds, insurance firms, and hedge funds. Growth in the institutional investor universe during the past ten years has been largely fueled by the growth in the hedge fund universe, representing over a trillion dollars of assets under management. As hedge funds seek to place capital to work in more sophisticated ways, the markets have evolved, with investment banks now offering more complex financial products than ever.

Fidelity, T. Rowe Price, Janus and other mutual fund companies represent a large portion of the buy-side business. Insurance companies like Prudential and Northwestern Mutual also manage large blocks of assets and are another segment of the buy-side. Yet another class of buy-side firms manage pension fund assets—frequently, a company's pension assets will be given to a specialty buy-side firm that can better manage the funds and hopefully generate higher returns than the company itself could have. There is substantial overlap among these money managers—some, such as Putnam and T. Rowe, manage both mutual funds for individuals as well as pension fund assets of large corporations.

Hedge Funds: What Exactly Are They?

Hedge funds are one sexy component of the buy-side. Since the mid-1990s, hedge funds' popularity has grown tremendously. Hedge funds pool together money from large investors (usually wealthy individuals) with the goal of making outsized gains. Historically, hedge funds bought individual stocks, and shorted (or borrowed against) the S&P 500 or another market index, as a hedge against the stock. (The funds bet against the S&P in order to reduce their risk.) As long as the individual stocks outperformed the S&P, the fund made money.

Nowadays, hedge funds have evolved into a myriad of high-risk money managers who essentially borrow money to invest in a multitude of stocks, bonds, loans, and derivative instruments (these funds with borrowed money are said to be "leveraged"). Essentially, a hedge fund uses its equity base to borrow substantially more capital, and therefore multiply its returns through this risky leveraging. Buying derivatives is a common way to quickly leverage a portfolio. Because hedge funds have relatively few (and wealthy) shareholders, they remain largely unregulated.

There are literally thousands of hedge funds; some of the most notable names are Citadel, D. E. Shaw, Highland Capital, and SAC Capital. As high-stakes money managers, many operate under the 2/20 rule, whereby 2% of the firms' capital under management is used to operate the fund and 20% of the gains are paid out to the fund's managers. Often times, the heads of these firms are the best-paid individuals on Wall Street, many of them personally earning hundreds of millions of dollars in recent years (it is rumored that Steven A. Cohen of SAC earned over $1 billion in 2005).

Visit the Vault Finance Career Channel at **www.vault.com/finance** – with insider firm profiles, message boards, the Vault Finance Job Board and more.

VAULT CAREER LIBRARY   19

Conversely, as the nature of the business is based on risk, quite often firms can collapse very quickly. Recently, the hedge fund industry has come under intense scrutiny from regulators after the implosion of the $9 billion fund of Amaranth Advisors. Many also recall the most famous hedge fund collapse as the meltdown of Long-Term Capital Management (LTCM) in 1998.

The Equity Markets

CHAPTER 3

"The Dow Jones Industrial Average added 38.93 points to 10,424.41, bolstered by a 1.2 percent gain in component Intel," The Wall Street Journal reported on November 11, 2004. The Journal also reported that Intel gains helped boost the NASDAQ Composite Index, but oil futures were on the decline again."

If you are new to the financial industry, you may be wondering exactly what all of these headlines mean and how to interpret them. The next two chapters are intended to provide a quick overview of the financial markets and what drives them, and introduce you to some market lingo as well. For reference, many definitions and explanations of many common types of securities can be found in the glossary at the end of this guide.

Bears vs. Bulls

Almost everyone loves a bull market, and an investor seemingly cannot go wrong when the market continues to reach new highs. At Goldman Sachs, a bull market is said to occur when stocks exhibit expanding multiples—we will give you a simpler definition. Essentially, a bull market occurs when stock prices (as measured by an index like the Dow Jones Industrial or the S&P 500) move up. A bear market occurs when stocks fall. Simple. More specifically, bear markets generally occur when the market has fallen by greater than 20 percent from its highs, and a correction occurs when the market has fallen by more than 10 percent but less than 20 percent. An easy way to remember this principle is that, when attacking, a bull strikes up and a bear strikes down.

The most widely publicized, most widely traded, and most widely tracked stock index in the world is the Dow Jones Industrial Average. The Dow was created in 1896 as a yardstick to measure the performance of the U.S. stock market in general. Initially composed of only 12 stocks, the Dow began trading at a mere 41 points. Today the Dow is made up of 30 large companies in a variety of industries and is measured in the thousands of points. Although the Dow is widely watched and cited because it's comprised of select, very large companies (known as "large caps"), the Dow cannot gauge fluctuations and movements in smaller companies (or "small caps").

In November 1999, the Dow Jones updated its composite, adding and removing companies to better reflect the current economy. Union Carbide, Goodyear Tire & Rubber, Sears, Roebuck & Co., and Chevron were removed. Microsoft, Intel, SBC Communications, and Home Depot were added. In 2004, more changes were made, as AT&T, Eastman Kodak and International Paper were replaced with AIG, Pfizer, and Verizon. Due to the merger of AT&T and SBC in late 2005, AT&T was re-added to the DJIA and SBC was removed.

The stocks in the following chart comprise the index as of the publication of this guide.

Components of the Dow Jones Industrial Average (as of 03/07)

American Express	General Motors	Microsoft
A.I.G	Hewlett-Packard	Pfizer
AT&T	Home Depot Inc	Procter & Gamble
Boeing	Honeywell International	United Technologies
Caterpillar	IBM	Verizon
Citigroup	Intel	Wal-Mart
Coca-Cola Co.	Johnson & Johnson	Walt Disney
Source: Dow Jones & Co.		

The Dow and NASDAQ

The Dow has historically performed remarkably well, particularly in the late 1990s. After a stumble in the late 1990s/early 2000s, it recovered to reach all-time highs in April 2007. In 1997, the Dow was hovering near 7000, before soaring above 11,000 points in 2000. However, after correcting to mid 7000s in 2003, the Dow began an upward surge to its newest highs, above 13,000.

Propelling the Dow throughout the late 1990s was an upward was a combination of the success of U.S. businesses in capturing productivity/efficiency gains, the continuing economic expansion, rapidly growing market share in world markets, and the U.S.'s global dominance in the expanding technology sectors. After a general economic downturn in 2001-2002, in addition to the 2001 terrorist attacks, the Dow retreated back to these early 1990 levels. However, record low borrowing rates, abundant corporate cash balances, low default rates (i.e. bankruptcies by companies), positive global economic data, and the rise of corporate profits have all contributed to the Dow's most recent surge.

The NASDAQ Composite garnered significant interest in the late 1990s years mainly because it was (and still is) driven largely by technology-related stocks. The NASDAQ stock market is an electronic market on which the stocks of many well-known technology companies (including Microsoft and Intel) trade. The acronym is short for the National Association of Securities Dealers Automated Quotations. Now, over 3,000 companies are listed on the stock exchange. In early 2000, the NASDAQ market became the first stock market to trade two billion shares in a single day. Interestingly, NASDAQ is owned by The Nasdaq Stock Market Inc, which trades on the NASDAQ exchange under the symbol NDAQ.

In early 2000, both the Dow and the NASDAQ were at record highs, but critics were wary of the end of the bull market. April 2000 was that end; both indices started a slow slide that lasted over a year and coincided with a general economic malaise. The indices' slow slide became a free-fall on September 17, 2001, the first day of trading after the terrorist attacks on the World Trade Center and the Pentagon. The Dow fell 7.13 percent, losing 684.81, the largest point drop ever. The NASDAQ was down 6.83 percent, or 115.83 points. The plunge is a good illustration of how outside events affect the stock markets; investors feared the economic impact of the attacks and the ensuing military response. It's worth noting that the markets reacted the same way after events of similar historical significance, including the bombing of Pearl Harbor and the assassination of President John F. Kennedy.

In 2003, for the first year since 1999, the Dow Jones Industrial Index finished on an uptick, gaining 25.3 percent and surpassing the 25.2 percent climb it made in 1999. The NASDAQ composite index also ended 2003 in solid fashion, increasing 50 percent during the year. Driving the gains in the market were low interest rates, a weaker dollar and low inventories. The only real downtick during the year, when stocks hit their lows, came in March during the outset of the war in Iraq.

Since this uptick in 2003, both indices have been on a long bull-market streak, with the Dow reaching record highs and the NASDAQ reaching levels not seen since 2001 (although still very far from its 2000 levels). In 2004, 2005, and 2006, the Dow returned approximately 3.1%, -0.6%, and 16.3%, while the NASDAQ returned approximately 8.6%, 1.4%, and 9.5%. As mentioned earlier, fueling this streak has been investor confidence, low interest rates, and positive economic sentiment throughout all major

Visit the Vault Finance Career Channel at www.vault.com/finance – with
insider firm profiles, message boards, the Vault Finance Job Board and more.

VAULT CAREER LIBRARY

23

financial markets worldwide. Many investors expect that after such a long bull run, both indices are due for a correction. However, with abundant investor cash balances, healthy corporate balance sheets, and positive economic indicators, the economy could have plenty of fuel left in its tank for an extended run.

A Word of Caution about the Dow

While the Dow may dominate news and conversation, investors should take care to know it has limitations as a market barometer. For one, the Dow can move be swiftly moved by changes in only one stock. Roughly speaking, for every dollar that any Dow component stock moves, the Dow Index will move by approximately four points. This is especially troubling, when considering the rise in oil prices over the past few years, that a stock such as Exxon (which has gone from roughly $30 per share in 2003 to nearly $80 in late 2006) has single-handedly fueled nearly 200 points of the Dow's growth. Also, the Dow is only composed of immense companies, and will only reflect movements in large-cap stocks. The Dow tends to have more psychological significance to individual investors than to professional investors, who tend to follow broader market indices.

Other benchmarks

Besides the Dow Jones and the NASDAQ Composite, investors follow many other important benchmarks. The NYSE Composite Index, which measures the performance of every stock traded on the New York Stock Exchange, represents an excellent broad market measure. The S&P 500 Index, composed of the 500 largest publicly traded companies in the U.S., also presents a widely followed broad market measure, but, like the Dow, is limited to large companies. The Russell 2000 compiles 2000 small-cap stocks, and measures stock performance in that segment of companies. Furthermore, with the rise in Exchange Traded Funds (ETFs), indices can be replicated and invested in, just like individual stocks. Note that Wall Street money managers tend to measure their performance against one of these market indices, not individual stocks.

Large-cap and small-cap

At a basic level, market capitalization or market cap represents the company's value according to the market and is calculated by multiplying the total number of shares by share price. (This is the equity value of the company.) Companies and their stocks tend to be categorized into three broad categories: large-cap, mid-cap, and small-cap.

While there are no hard and fast rules, generally speaking, a company with a market cap greater than $5 billion will be classified as a large-cap stock. These companies tend to be established, mature companies, although with some IPOs rising rapidly, this is not necessarily the case. Sometimes huge companies with $100 billion and greater market caps, for example, GE (~$380 billion) and Microsoft (~$300 billion), are called mega-cap stocks. Small-cap stocks tend to be riskier, but are also often the faster growing companies. Roughly speaking, small-cap stocks include those companies with market caps less than $1 billion. And as one might expect, the stocks in between $1 billion and $5 billion are referred to as mid-cap stocks.

What moves the stock market?

Not surprisingly, the factors that most influence the broader stock market are economic in nature. Among equities, corporate profits and interest rates are king.

Corporate profits: When Gross Domestic Product slows substantially, market investors fear a recession and a drop in corporate profits. And if economic conditions worsen and the market enters a recession, many companies will face reduced demand for their products, company earnings will be hurt, and hence equity (stock) prices will decline. Thus, when the GDP suffers, so does the stock market.

Interest rates: When the Consumer Price Index heats up, investors fear inflation. Inflation fears trigger a different chain of events than fears of recession. Most importantly, inflation will cause interest rates to rise. Companies with debt will be forced to pay higher interest rates on existing debt, thereby reducing earnings (and earnings per share). Compounding the problem, because inflation fears cause interest rates to rise, higher rates will make investments other than stocks more attractive from the investor's perspective. Why would an investor purchase a stock that may only earn 8 percent (and carries substantial risk), when lower risk CDs and government bonds offer similar yields with less risk? These inflation fears are known as capital allocations in the market (whether investors are putting money into stocks vs. bonds), which can substantially impact stock and bond prices. Investors typically re-allocate funds from stocks to low-risk bonds when the economy experiences a slowdown and vice-versa when the opposite occurs.

Visit the Vault Finance Career Channel at www.vault.com/finance – with insider firm profiles, message boards, the Vault Finance Job Board and more.

VAULT CAREER LIBRARY

25

What moves *individual* stocks?

When it comes to individual stocks, it's all about earnings, earnings, earnings. No other measure even compares to earnings per share (EPS) when it comes to an individual stock's price. Every quarter, public companies must report EPS figures, and stockholders wait with bated breath, ready to compare the actual EPS figure with the EPS estimates set by Wall Street research analysts (which are set from their continued conversations with the company). For instance, if a company reports $1.00 EPS for a quarter, but the market had anticipated EPS of $1.20, the stock will almost certainly be dramatically hit in the market by a sell-off during the next trading day. Conversely, a company that beats its estimates will typically rally in the markets. Earnings per share are often adjusted for unforeseen events, such as one-time charges, which allow investors to evaluate whether or not the core business of a firm is growing or declining.

It is important to note at this point, that in the frenzied Internet stock market of 1999 and early 2000, investors did not show the traditional focus on near-term earnings. It was acceptable for many small technology companies to operate at a loss for a year or more, because these companies, investors hoped, would achieve long term future earnings. As investors believed these long term substantial earnings would translate into high eventual EPS, they continued to purchase the stocks, driving up the stock prices. However, when the markets turned in the spring of 2000, investors began to expect even "new economy" companies to demonstrate more substantial near-term earnings capacity. For many companies, this did not happen.

For anything other than comparison purposes, the market does not care about last year's earnings or even last quarter's earnings. What matters most to an investor is what will happen in the near future. Investors maintain a tough, "what have you done for me lately" attitude, and forgive slowly a company that consistently fails to meet analysts' estimates ("misses its numbers").

Stock Valuation Measures and Ratios

As far as stocks go, it is important to realize that absolute stock prices mean nothing. A $100 stock could be "cheaper" than a $10 stock. To clarify how this works, consider the following ratios and what they mean. Keep in mind that these are only a few of the major ratios, and that literally hundreds of financial and accounting ratios have been invented to compare dissimilar companies. Again, it is important to note that most of these ratios were not as applicable in the market's evaluation of certain Internet and technology stocks in the late 1990s.

P/E ratio

You can't go far into a discussion about the stock market without hearing about the all-important price to earnings ratio, or P/E ratio. By definition, a P/E ratio equals the stock price divided by the earnings per share. Investors use the P/E ratio to indicate how cheap or expensive a stock is. Consider the following example. Two similar firms each have $1.50 in EPS. Company A's stock price is $15.00 per share, and Company B's stock price is $30.00 per share.

Company	Stock Price	Earnings Per Share	P/E Ratio
A	$ 15.00	$1.50	10x
B	$ 30.00	$1.50	20x

Clearly, Company A is cheaper than Company B with regard to the P/E ratio because both firms exhibit the same level of earnings, but A's stock trades at a higher price. That is, Company A's P/E ratio of 10 (15/1.5) is lower than Company B's P/E ratio of 20 (30/1.5). Hence, Company A's stock trades at a lower price. The terminology one hears in the market is, "Company A is trading at 10 times earnings, while Company B is trading at 20 times earnings." Twenty times is a higher multiple.

However, the true measure of cheapness vs. richness cannot be summed up by the P/E ratio. Some firms simply deserve higher P/E ratios than others, and some deserve lower P/Es. Importantly, the distinguishing factor is the anticipated growth in earnings per share.

PEG ratio

Because companies grow at different rates, another comparison investors often make is between the P/E ratio and the stock's expected growth rate in EPS. Returning to our previous example, let's say Company A has an expected EPS growth rate of 10 percent, while Company B's expected growth rate is 20 percent.

Company	Stock Price	Earnings Per Share	P/E Ratio	Estimated Growth Rate in EPS
A	$ 15.00	$1.50	10x	10x
B	$ 30.00	$1.50	20x	20x

We might propose that the market values Company A at 10 times earnings because it anticipates 10 percent annual growth in EPS over the next five years. Company B is growing faster—at a 20 percent rate—and therefore justifies the 20 times earnings stock price. To determine true cheapness, market analysts have developed a ratio that compares the P/E to the growth rate—the PEG ratio. In this example, one could argue that both companies are priced similarly (both have PEG ratios of 1).

Sophisticated market investors therefore utilize this PEG ratio rather than just the P/E ratio. Roughly speaking, the average company has a PEG ratio of 1:1 or 1 (i.e., the P/E ratio matches the anticipated growth rate). By convention, "expensive" firms have a PEG ratio greater than one, and "cheap" stocks have a PEG ratio less than one.

Cash flow multiples

For companies with no earnings (or losses) and therefore no EPS (or negative EPS), one cannot calculate the P/E ratio—it is a meaningless number. An alternative is to compute the firm's cash flow and compare that to the market value of the firm. The following example illustrates how a typical cash flow multiple like Enterprise Value/EBITDA ratio is calculated.

> **EBITDA**: A proxy for cash flow, EBITDA stands for Earnings Before Interest, Taxes, Depreciation and Amortization. To calculate EBITDA, work your way up the Income Statement, adding back the appropriate items to net income. Depreciation and amortization are added back, as they are not actual cash-based costs. Taxes are added back, because

taxes are paid only if a company is profitable after it has paid for everything else. Interest is added back too, as it is paid on existing debt, for which the cash flow could potentially be used to do other things. (Note: For a more detailed explanation of this and other financial calculations, see the Vault Guide to Finance Interviews.) Adding together depreciation and amortization to operating earnings, a common subtotal on the income statement, can serve as a shortcut to calculating EBITDA.

Enterprise value (EV) = market value of equity + net debt. To compute market value of equity, simply multiply the current stock price times the number of shares outstanding. Net debt is simply the firm's total debt (as found on the balance sheet) minus cash.

Enterprise value to revenue multiple (EV/revenue)

If you follow startup companies or young technology or healthcare related companies, you have probably heard the multiple of revenue lingo. Sometimes it is called the price-sales ratio (though this technically is not correct). Why use this ratio? For one, many firms not only have negative earnings, but also negative cash flow. That means any cash flow or P/E multiple must be thrown out the window, leaving revenue as the last positive income statement number left to compare to the firm's enterprise value. Specifically one calculates this ratio by dividing EV by the last 12 months revenue figure.

Return on equity (ROE)

ROE = Net income divided by total shareholder's equity. ROE is an important measure, especially for financial services companies, which evaluates the return on income that a firm earned in any given year. Return on equity is expressed as a percentage. Many firms' financial goal is to achieve a certain level of ROE per year, say 20 percent or more.

Basic Equity Definitions

Common stock: Also called common equity, common stock represents an ownership interest in a company. The vast majority of stock traded in the markets today is common. Common stock enables investors to vote on company matters.

Convertible preferred stock: This is a relatively uncommon type of equity issued by a company, often when it cannot successfully sell either straight common stock or straight debt. Convertible preferred stock usually pays dividends in a manner similar to the way a bond pays coupon payments. However, preferred stock ultimately converts to common stock after a period of time. Preferred stock can be viewed as a mix of debt and equity, and is most often used as a way for a risky company to obtain capital when neither debt nor equity works. In terms of its relative priority on the claim of the assets of a company in the event of a bankruptcy, preferred stock is higher on the food chain than common stock.

Non-convertible preferred stock: Sometimes companies (usually those with steady and predictable earnings) issue non-convertible preferred stock that pays steady dividends. This stock remains outstanding in perpetuity and trades similar to bonds. Utilities represent the best example of non-convertible preferred stock issuers.

Value Stocks, Growth Stocks and Momentum Investors

It is important to know that investors typically classify stocks into one of two categories – growth and value stocks. Momentum investors buy a subset of the stocks in the growth category.

Value stocks are those that often have been battered by investors. Typically, a stock that trades at low P/E ratios after having once traded at high P/E's, or a stock with declining sales or earnings fits into the value category. Investors choose value stocks with the hope that their businesses will turn around and profits will return. Or, investors perhaps realize that a stock is trading close to or even below its "break-up value" (net proceeds upon liquidation of the company), and hence have little downside.

Growth stocks are just the opposite. High P/E's, high growth rates, and often hot stocks fit the growth category. Technology stocks, with sometimes astoundingly high P/E's, may be classified as growth stocks, based on their high growth potential. Keep in mind that a P/E ratio often serves as a proxy for a firm's average expected growth rate, because as discussed, investors will generally pay a high P/E for a faster growing company.

Momentum investors buy growth stocks that have exhibited strong upward price appreciation. Usually trading at or near their "52-week highs" (the highest trading price during the previous two weeks), momentum investors cause these stocks to trade up and down with extreme volatility. Momentum investors, who typically don't care much about the firm's business or valuation ratios, will dump their stocks the moment they show price weakness. Thus, a stock run-up by momentum investors can potentially crash dramatically as investors bail out at the first sign of trouble.

Visit the Vault Finance Career Channel at **www.vault.com/finance** — with insider firm profiles, message boards, the Vault Finance Job Board and more.

VAULT CAREER LIBRARY

31

How many consulting job boards have you visited lately?

(Thought so.)

Use the Internet's most targeted

job search tools for consulting

professionals.

Vault Consulting Job Board

The most comprehensive and convenient job board for consulting professionals. Target your search by area of consulting, function, and experience level, and find the job openings that you want. No surfing required.

VaultMatch Resume Database

Vault takes match-making to the next level: post your resume and customize your search by area of consulting, experience and more. We'll match job listings with your interests and criteria and e-mail them directly to your inbox.

The Debt Markets

CHAPTER 4

An Introduction to Debt

Debt is everywhere. From credit cards to small business loans to multi-billion dollar bond issuances, debt is an integral part of the financial markets. Most everyone in the world has access to some form of debt. Although it normally has a negative connotation, debt is also the most common way for a company to raise capital. Most companies are simply too small (or do not want) to have public equity and be traded in the stock markets. Therefore, they opt for loans, bonds, or another form of debt to fill their day-to-day funding needs.

For the average person, the debt markets are not as visible, nor as easy to understand as the equity market. In fact, despite this low profile, the debt markets are substantially larger than the equity markets. Even the bond market, which is just a subset of the overall debt market, is larger than the equity market.

Historically, the debt markets were synonymous with "fixed income," or products that had a fixed return, year over year (i.e. a bond's coupon payments). However, in the past decade, as the syndicated loan market has grown and evolved, the debt markets have become both fixed and floating income markets. Now, many refer to the overall debt markets as the "credit markets," which refers to an even larger umbrella that not only includes loans and bonds, as well as other related fixed income securities (ABS, MBS, etc.), but also the corresponding debt-related derivative instruments (CLOs, CDOs, Credit Default Swaps and Structured Credit). However, be aware that both the loan and bond markets (including securitizations) comprise the vast majority of the debt markets.

What is the Bond Market?

Until the late 1970s and early 80s, bonds were considered not very attractive investments, bought by retired grandparents, retirement funds, and insurance companies. They traded infrequently, and provided safe, steady returns. The term "clipping coupons" actually refers to retirees using the coupon payments from their bonds as income.

Beginning in the early 1980s, however, Wharton graduate and former Wall Street golden boy Michael Milken essentially created the "junk bond" financial market, while amassing a large fortune at the same time. This market would go on to create a number of other financial markets, and today still brings nearly $100 billion of annual new issuance of bonds to investors. With the development of mortgage-backed securities, Salomon Brothers also contributed to the bond market evolution, transforming bonds into something exciting and extremely profitable for investment banks.

To begin our discussion of the fixed income portion of the debt market, we'll identify the main types of securities that comprise it. We'll discuss some of these more in-depth throughout the chapter.

- U.S. Government Treasury securities
- Agency bonds
- High grade corporate bonds
- High yield (junk) bonds
- Municipal bonds
- Mortgage-backed bonds
- Asset-backed securities
- Emerging market bonds
- CDOs/CLOs

Bond Market Indicators

The yield curve

Bond "yields" are the current rate of return to an investor who buys the bond. (Yield is measured in "basis points"; each basis point = 1/100 of one percent.) A primary measure of importance to fixed income investors is the yield curve. The yield curve (also called the "term structure of interest rates") depicts graphically the yields on different maturity U.S. government securities. To construct a simple yield curve, investors typically look at the yield on a 90-day U.S. T-bill and then the yield on the 30-year U.S. government bond (called the Long Bond). Typically, the yields of shorter-term government T-bill are lower than Long Bond's yield, indicating what is called an "upward sloping yield curve." This is fairly intuitive, because as an investor, you would expect more return for your money if it were locked up in a longer-term investment. Sometimes, short-term interest rates are higher than long-term rates, creating what is known as an "inverse yield curve."

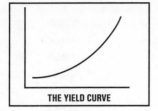

THE YIELD CURVE

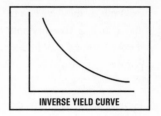

INVERSE YIELD CURVE

Bond indices

As with the stock market, the bond market has some widely watched indexes of its own. One prominent example is the Lehman Government Corporate Bond Index ("LGC"). The LGC index measures the returns on mostly government securities, but also blends in a portion of corporate bonds. The index is adjusted periodically to reflect the percentage of assets in government and in corporate bonds in the market. Mortgage bonds are excluded entirely from the LGC index.

U.S. government bonds

Particularly important in the universe of fixed income products are U.S. government bonds. These bonds are the most reliable in the world, as the

U.S. government is unlikely to default on its loans because it can essentially print money to meet its debt obligations. However, if it ever did default, the world financial markets would essentially be in shambles. Because they are virtually risk-free, U.S. government bonds, also called Treasuries, offer relatively low yields (a low rate of interest), and are the standards by which other bond yields are measured. If a financial ratio refers to the "risk-free rate of return", it is usually referring to a specific U.S. Government Treasury security.

Spreads

In the bond world, investors track "spreads" as carefully as any single index of bond prices or any single bond. The spread is essentially the difference between a specific bond's yield (the amount of interest, measured in percent, paid to bondholders), and the yield on a U.S. Treasury bond of the same time to maturity. For instance, an investor investigating the 20-year Acme Corp. bond would compare it to a U.S. Treasury bond that has 20 years remaining until maturity. Because U.S. Treasury bonds are considered to have zero risk of default, a corporation's bond will always trade at a yield that is over the yield on a comparable Treasury bond. For example, if the Acme Corp. 10-year bond traded at a yield of 8.4 percent and a 10-year Treasury note was trading at 8 percent, a trader would say that the Acme bond was trading at "40 over" (here, the "40" refers to 40 basis points).

Bond ratings for corporate and municipal bonds

A bond's risk level, or the risk that the bond issuer will default on payments to bondholders, is measured by bond rating agencies. Several companies rate credit, but Standard & Poor's and Moody's are the two largest. The riskier a bond, the larger the spread: low-risk bonds trade at a small spread to Treasuries, while below-investment grade bonds trade at tremendous spreads to Treasuries. Investors refer to company specific risk as credit risk.

Triple A ratings represents the highest possible corporate bond designation, and are reserved for the best-managed, largest blue-chip companies. Triple A bonds trade at a yield close to the yield on a risk-free government Treasury. Junk bonds, or bonds with a rating of BB or below on the S&P scale, currently trade at yields ranging from 15 percent, depending on the precise rating and government bond interest rates at the time.

Companies continue to be monitored by the rating agencies as long as their bonds trade in the markets. If a company is put on "credit watch," it is possible that the rating agencies are considering raising or lowering the rating on the company. Often an agency will put a company's bonds on credit watch "with positive or negative implications," giving investors a preview of which way any future change will go. When a bond is actually downgraded by Moody's or S&P, the bond's price drops dramatically (and therefore its yield increases).

The following table summarizes rating symbols of the two major rating agencies and provides a brief definition of each. It is important to note that at each major rating grade of S&P, there are + and -'s given to individual ratings. Thus, a bond could have a BB+, BB, or BB- rating. As with Moody's, this distinction is made with a 1,2, or 3 scale, such that a bond could have a Ba1, Ba2, or Ba3 rating. The precise cutoff of investment grade bonds would be anything with a BB+ or lower rating from S&P or a Ba1 or lower rating from Moody's. If a bond has obtained an investment grade rating from one agency and a high-yield rating from another, it is referred to as a "crossover credit" and usually falls into the world of high-yield bonds.

Bond Rating Codes

Rating	S & P	Moody's
Highest quality	AAA	Aaa
High quality	AA	Aa
Upper medium quality	A	A
Medium grade	BBB	Baa
Somewhat speculative	BB	Ba
Low grade, speculative	B	B
Low grade, default possible	CCC	Caa
Low grade, partial recovery possible	CC	Ca
Default expected	C	C

Source: Moody's Investor's Service and Standard and Poor's

Factors affecting the bond market

What factors affect the bond market? In short, interest rates. The general level of interest rates, as measured by many different barometers (see inset) moves bond prices up and down, in dramatic inverse fashion. In other words, if interest rates rise, the bond markets suffer.

Think of it this way. Say you own a bond that is paying you a fixed rate of 8 percent today, and that this rate represents a 1.5 percent spread over Treasuries. An increase in rates of 1 percent means that this same bond purchased now (as opposed to when you purchased the bond) will now yield 9 percent. And as the yield goes up, the price declines. So, your bond loses value and you are only earning 8 percent when the rest of the market is earning 9 percent.

You could have waited, purchased the bond after the rate increase, and earned a greater yield. The opposite occurs when rates go down. If you lock in a fixed rate of 8 percent and rates plunge by 1 percent, you now earn more than those who purchase the bond after the rate decrease. Therefore, as interest rates change the price or value of bonds will rise or fall so that all comparable bonds will trade at the same yield regardless of when or at what interest rate these bonds were issued.

Why do interest rates move?

Interest rates react mostly to inflation expectations (expectations of a rise in prices). If it is believed that inflation will rise, then interest rates rise. Think of it this way. Say inflation is 5 percent a year. In order to make money on a loan, a bank would have to at least charge more than 5 percent—otherwise it would essentially be losing money on the loan. The same is true with bonds and other fixed income products.

In the late 1970s, interest rates topped 20 percent, as inflation began to spiral out of control (and the market expected continued high inflation). Today, many believe that the Federal Reserve has successfully slayed inflation and has all but eliminated market concerns of this amount of future inflation, at least in the near term. This is certainly debatable, but clearly, the sound monetary policies and remarkable price stability in the U.S. have made it the envy of many other financial markets around the world.

Which Interest Rate Are You Talking About?

Investment banking professionals often discuss interest rates in general terms. But what are they really talking about? So many rates are tossed about that they may be difficult to track. To clarify, we will take a brief look at the key rates worth tracking. We have ranked them in typically ascending order: the discount rate usually is the lowest rate; the yield on junk bonds is usually the highest.

The discount rate: The discount rate is the rate that the Federal Reserve charges on overnight loans to banks. Today, the discount rate can be directly changed by the Fed, but maintains a largely symbolic role.

Federal funds rate: The rate domestic banks charge one another on overnight loans to meet Federal Reserve requirements. This rate is also directly controlled by the Fed and is a critical interest rate to financial markets.

T-Bill yields: The yield or internal rate of return an investor would receive at any given moment on a 90- to 360-day Treasury bill.

LIBOR (London Interbank Offered Rate): Derived from the rate banks in England charge one another on overnight loans or loans up to five years. Often used by banks to quote floating rate loan interest rates. Typically, the benchmark LIBOR used on loans is the three-month rate.

The Long Bond (30-Year Treasury) yield: The yield or internal rate of return an investor would receive at any given moment on the 30-year U.S. Treasury bond.

Municipal bond yields: The yield or internal rate of return an investor would receive at any given moment by investing in municipal bonds. We should note that the interest on municipal bonds typically is free from federal government taxes and therefore has a lower yield than other bonds of similar risk. These yields, however, can vary substantially depending on their rating, so could be higher or lower than presented here.

High grade corporate bond yield: The yield or internal rate of return an investor would receive by purchasing a corporate bond with a rating above BB.

Prime rate: The average rate that U.S. banks charge to companies for loans.

30-year mortgage rates: The average interest rate on 30-year home mortgages. Mortgage rates typically move in line with the yield on the 10-year Treasury note.

High yield bonds: The yield or internal rate of return an investor would receive by purchasing a corporate bond with a rating below BBB (also called junk bonds).

A Note About the Federal Reserve

The Federal Reserve Bank, called the Fed and headed by Ben Bernanke (formerly headed by Alan Greenspan), monitors the U.S. money supply and regulates banking institutions. The Fed's role is crucial to the U.S. economy and stock market.

Academic studies of economic history have shown that a country's inflation rate tends to track that country's increase in its money supply. Therefore, if the Fed allows the money supply to increase by 2 percent this year, inflation can best be predicted to increase by about 2 percent as well. Because inflation so dramatically impacts the stock and bond markets, the markets scrutinize the daily activities of the Fed and hang onto every word uttered by Bernanke.

Visit the Vault Finance Career Channel at **www.vault.com/finance** – with
insider firm profiles, message boards, the Vault Finance Job Board and more.

VAULT CAREER LIBRARY   39

The Fed can manage consumption patterns and hence the GDP by raising or lowering interest rates.

The chain of events when the Fed raises rates is as follows:

> The Fed raises interest rates. This interest rate increase triggers banks to raise interest rates, which leads to consumers and businesses borrowing less and spending less. This decrease in consumption tends to slow down GDP, thereby reducing earnings at companies. Since consumers and businesses borrow less, they have left their money in the bank and hence the money supply does not expand. Note also that since companies tend to borrow less when rates go up, they therefore typically invest less in capital equipment, which discourages productivity gains and hurts earnings of capital goods providers. Any economist will tell you that a key to a growing economy on a per capita basis is improving labor productivity.

Fixed Income Definitions

The following glossary may be useful for defining securities that trade in the markets as well as talking about the factors that influence them. Note that this is just a list of the most common types of fixed income products and economic indicators. Thousands of fixed income products actually trade in the markets.

Types of Securities	
Treasury securities	United States government-issued securities. Categorized as Treasury bills (maturity of up to—but not including—two years), Treasury notes (from two years to 10 years maturity), and Treasury bonds (10 years to 30 years). As they are government-guaranteed, Treasuries are considered "risk-free." In fact, U.S. Treasuries have no default risk, but do have interest rate risk—if rates increase, then the price of US Treasuries issued in the past will decrease.
Agency bonds	Agencies represent all bonds issued by the federal government and federal agencies, but excluding those issued by the Treasury (i.e., bonds issued by other agencies of the federal government). Examples of agencies that issue bonds include Federal National Mortgage Association (FNMA) and Guaranteed National Mortgage Association (GNMA).
Investment grade (high grade) corporate bonds	Bonds with a Standard & Poor's rating of at least a BBB-. Typically big, blue-chip companies issue highly rated bonds.
High yield (junk) bonds	Bonds with a Standard & Poor's rating lower than BBB-. Typically smaller, riskier companies issue high yield bonds.
Municipal bonds	Bonds issued by local and state governments, a.k.a. municipalities. Municipal bond income is tax-free for the investor, which means investors in "muni's" earn interest payments without having to pay federal taxes. Sometimes investors are exempt from state and local taxes too. Consequently, municipalities can pay lower interest rates on muni bonds than other bonds of similar risk.

Types of Securities

Money market securities	The market for securities (typically corporate, but also Treasury securities) maturing within one year, including short-term CDs, Repurchase Agreements, and Commercial Paper (low-risk corporate issues), among others. These are low-risk, short-term securities that have yields similar to Treasuries.
Mortgage-backed bonds	Bonds collateralized by a pool of mortgages. Interest and principal payments are based on the individual homeowners making their mortgage payments. The more diverse the pool of mortgages backing the bond, the less risky they are typically considered.
Collateralized Debt Obligation	A structured credit product comprised of different tranches of debt. Pays an interest rate based on the tranches of debt comprising the security.

Economic Indicators

Gross Domestic Product	GDP measures the total domestic output of goods and services in the United States. Generally, when the GDP grows at a rate of less than 2%, the economy is considered to be in an economic slowdown; negative growth, or shrinkage, indicates recession.
Consumer Price Index	The CPI measures the percentage increase in the price for goods and services. Essentially, the CPI measures inflation affecting consumers.
Producer Price Index	The PPI measures the percentage increase in the price of a standard basket of goods and services. PPI is a measure of inflation for producers and manufacturers.

Economic Indicators

Unemployment Rate and Wages	In 1999 through early 2000, U.S. unemployment was at record lows. Clearly, this was a positive sign for the U.S. economy because jobs are plentiful. The markets sometimes react negatively to extremely low levels of unemployment, since, as a tight labor market means that firms may have to raise wages (called wage pressure). Substantial wage pressure may force firms to raise prices, and hence may cause inflation to flare up. Marked increases in unemployment are seen as a sign of economic weakness, and can be a symptom of a slowdown or recession.

What is the Loan Market?

Club: It's not just a great sandwich

There are three general categories of loans: bilateral, club, and syndicated. Bilateral, the traditional loan, refers to a loan between one lender and one company or individual. These loans usually exist only for small companies and individuals. "Club" refers to loans between a small group of lenders (usually from two to five) and a company. Like bilateral loans, these loans do not undergo a syndication process and do not usually trade in the markets. Finally, there are syndicated loans, which comprise the vast majority of the loan market. These are loans provided by numerous institutions for a single company.

The Syndicated Loan Market

The syndicated loan market is one of the largest asset classes in the world. It originated out of the simple concept of bank lending and has grown over time in response to companies and their financial needs. Today, annual issuance volume in the loan market is near $1.5 trillion dollars. Yet the general public knows very little about the loan market. As loans are private and thus not registered with the SEC, information about a company's outstanding loans can usually only be found listed on a company's balance sheet under "credit facilities." However, the loan market bears a striking resemblance to its counterpart, the bond market.

Loans and bonds are both forms of debt, issued by companies to raise money. They are both quoted with spreads in relation to a risk-free instrument. They are both usually rated by Moody's and S&P and they are both either considered "high grade" or "high yield" by investors, depending on their ratings (however, a high yield loan is generally referred to as a "leveraged" loan). Both loans and bonds require an offering process (for bonds, this is the roadshow process, for loans this is usually a lenders' presentation) and they are both marketed to institutional investors. Although bond trading is currently more liquid than loans, both bonds and loans also trade actively in the financial markets.

However, this is about where most of the major similarities between the markets stop. While bonds are quoted as a fixed rate (say, an 8% bond), loans are quoted as a floating rate above LIBOR (say, L+225bps). Much like a bond, this rate, or spread of 225bps, essentially represents the corresponding risk of the underlying firm (i.e. "credit risk"). While bonds are SEC-registered, loans currently remain private instruments and are not. Also, loans are often times "secured," which means that they have the very first claim on a firm's assets in the event the company is liquidated. Bonds are generally not secured.

Although there are many other nuances to loans versus bonds, the quick takeaway is that both markets are very important markets for investors. For example, it is rumored that legendary Dallas-based hedge fund Highland Capital has over $30 billion in loan investments alone. Remember that while individuals have credit cards and home loans, so do companies. The only difference is that the company loans are usually significantly larger and have multiple lenders.

The products

Most large companies have "credit facilities" listed on their balance sheets. Usually, this refers to a package of loans they have outstanding, coming in the form of revolving credit facilities and term loans. Usually issued in conjunction with one another, it is not uncommon for a company to have both an RC and term loan. But it is uncommon (but definitely not unheard of) for companies to have multiple RCs or multiple term loans.

Revolving credit facility

Very similar to a credit card, these facilities function like a company's credit card. They have an annual fee (an undrawn fee and an administration fee), as well as a cost of borrowing, similar to an APR (a fully-drawn fee). If you think of your credit card, you are charged an interest rate on any balances you keep; the same is true of an RC. Along this same train of thought, leveraged clients tend to draw down on their RCs more than investment-grade clients, who tend to keep them for backup purposes. RCs usually are 5-7 years in length and are generally provided by a syndicate of commercial banks.

Term loan

If RCss are like credit cards, term loans can be thought of like an auto loan. Typically 5-7 years in length, term loans are fully-funded instruments purchased by investors. There are two main types of term loans: the "bank loan" (term loan A) and the institutional term loan (term loan B, C, D, etc). Think of the type of term loan as derived from its buyers. "Bank loans," as they are sometimes called, are purchased generally by commercial banks, are usually issued by investment grade (read: not risky) clients, are not secured by assets, and are not frequently traded in the markets. "Institutional term loans" are issued by leveraged companies, are purchased by institutional investors, have higher spreads than RCs and TL As, are usually secured by a company's assets, and are frequently traded in the markets.

2nd lien loan

Most similar to a bond, 2nd lien loans are a type of term loan that exists when a company already has another term loan outstanding. Basically, this means that in the event of liquidation, investors holding the 2nd lien loan must wait for the first-lien loans (RCs and term loans, which are generally pari passu) to be paid out before they have a claim on the company's assets. As in the case of a bond, this means that the loans pay investors a slightly higher spread for this increased risk tolerance. However, unlike bonds, these 2nd lien loans are often still secured by a company's assets.

The players

Finally, it's important to note that many investment banks have large groups dedicated solely to executing high yield bond and leveraged loan transactions for clients. These groups are usually referred to as a firm's leveraged finance platform, and they are responsible for completing some of the most premier transactions on Wall Street, including LBOs, dividends, recapitalizations, and restructurings. All of the major investment banks have established leveraged finance operations.

The firms with the largest leveraged finance presence dominate the issuance volume in the high yield bond and leveraged loan markets. In 2005, JPMorgan was the first firm ever to achieve a #1 ranking in both of these markets. Other firms with substantial leveraged finance operations include Bank of America, Citibank, CSFB, Deutsche Bank, Goldman Sachs, and Wachovia.

The roles

Much like bonds, investment banking roles in the syndicate loan market include arrangers, underwriters, and co-managers. These are covered in more detail in Chapter 11: Syndicate: The Go-Betweens.

For more information on the syndicated loan market, check out the Vault Career Guide to Leveraged Finance.

Trends In I-Banking

CHAPTER 5

What's the big deal?

Recent years have seen the return of the big bank merger. First was the October 2003 announcement that Bank of America would be acquiring FleetBoston for approximately $49 billion. In accepting the offer to merge, FleetBoston's chairman and CEO Charles "Chad" Gifford said that "it became increasingly clear to us that scale is a tremendous advantage, if properly managed," adding that "Bank of America was the one bank that was taking advantage of this scale." At the time, it looked like the large-scale merger would create the second-biggest U.S. banking firm behind Citigroup and JPMorgan Chase. But much to the chagrin of BofA, a couple of months later, in January 2004, JPMorgan Chase announced it would be acquiring Bank One in a deal worth more than $58 billion, at the time solidifying JPMorgan Chase's spot as the second-largest bank in the U.S. The transaction gave perennial No.1 Citigroup a run for its money, as the Bank One acquisition created a financial services giant with $1.1 trillion in assets, rivaling Citi's $1.2 trillion.

Determined not to be left out of the merger madness, Wachovia Corporation, the fourth-largest banking firm in the U.S., agreed to pay $14.3 billion to acquire SouthTrust Corporation in June 2004. The transaction gave the Charlotte, N.C.-based Wachovia a significantly stronger foothold in the Southeast.

As of March 2007, these banks are still the largest in the U.S., with Citigroup as #1 in market capitalization and assets ($245 billion and $1.88 trillion, respectively), Bank of America as #2 ($222.4 billion and $1.46 trillion), and JPMorgan Chase as #3 ($164 billion and $1.35 trillion).

A Record Year for M&A

As well as working on their own mergers, banks had their hands full with other firms' combinations in 2006. A record year for M&A, according to Thomson Financial, $3.8 trillion worth of mergers and acquisitions were announced globally in 2006, an increase of 38% over 2005 and a new global record over the previous high of $3.4 trillion in 2000. U.S. M&A comprised $1.6 trillion of this volume, up 36% from $1.2 trillion in 2005.

To put this bull market M&A surge in perspective, in 2003 there was only $523 billion of M&A activity in the U.S. In 2006, U.S. Financial Sponsor

M&A volume alone accounted for nearly $415 billion, or almost all of 2003's U.S. M&A volume. Notably, of all major clients, Financial Sponsors accounted for the largest percentage of transactions, comprising 20% of global M&A volume and 27% of U.S. volume. These came in the form of LBO transactions, five of which topped $25 billion each (Equity Office Properties Trust at $33 billion, HCA at $32 billion, Kinder Morgan at $28 billion, Harrah's Entertainment at $27 billion, and Clear Channel Communications at $27 billion). Not surprisingly, Financial Sponsors, M&A, and leveraged finance groups within investment banks have remained the hot places on Wall Street.

As for M&A timing, the fourth quarter was again the most active both globally and in the U.S., comprising 34% and 36% of the year's volume, respectively. Although a number of substantial transactions were completed during the fourth quarter, the largest in the U.S. was the acquisition of BellSouth by AT&T Corp in March 2006. Accounting for $89 billion of volume alone, this transaction was a hallmark deal for all investment banks involved. With the help of this transaction, both Goldman and Citigroup topped over $1 trillion of M&A advisory in 2006.

In terms of industry sectors, Energy and Power was the most active, both globally and in the Americas. Spurred by LBO activity in the E&P space, the sector had $600 billion of global M&A activity and nearly $256 billion of M&A activity in the Americas. Two major deals drove volume in this sector, including the aforementioned Kinder Morgan $28 billion LBO, and the $18 billion acquisition of Kerr-McGee by Anadarko.

As for league table standings, the top four firms held the top spots, both globally and in the Americas. According to Thomson Financial, globally, Goldman retained the #1 ranking (with $1.088 trillion of volume for 438 deals), with Citigroup at #2 ($1.034 trillion of volume for 417 deals), Morgan Stanley at #3 ($975 billion of volume for 299 deals), and JPMorgan at #4 (with $890 billion of volume for 437 deals). In the Americas, Goldman was also #1 (with $563 billion of volume for 192 deals), Citi was #2 ($438 of volume for 147 deals), JPMorgan was #3 ($414 billion of volume for 172 deals), and Morgan Stanley was #4 ($407 billion of volume for 149 deals).

This white-hot market translated into substantially increased M&A fees for all of the top players in 2006. As calculated by Freeman & Co. and reported by Thomson Financial, imputed global M&A fees were up 27% in 2006 from 2005, reaching $33 billion. In the U.S., these fees were up 24%, reaching $10.4 billion. Goldman, Morgan Stanley, and JPMorgan were the fee leaders, both globally and in the U.S.

Don't write off the underwriting

With the global financial markets hot as ever, global underwriters were a major force yet again, setting an annual record of bringing to market $7.64 trillion in debt, equity and equity-related deals, according to Thomson Financial. This rise of $1.028 trillion represented an increase of 16% over 2005 totals. Taking the top two spots yet again in global underwriting were Citigroup and JPMorgan, which booked $667 billion and $506 billion in debt, equity and equity-related deals in 2006, respectively. Deutsche Bank, with approximately $475 billion, took third place. According to Thomson Financial, as of the fourth quarter of 2006, Citigroup has maintained its #1 debt position for 21 straight quarters.

In the increasingly competitive arena of global equity and equity-related underwriting, which set an all-time record of $695 billion in total transaction volume in 2006 versus $526 billion in 2005, Goldman Sachs kept its narrow lead, with $67 billion of volume. Citigroup held on to No. 2 with $61 billion and Morgan Stanley was No. 3, with $57 billion. To put this market surge in perspective, the same global volume was a mere $388 billion in 2003, representing a 79% volume increase in just three years' time. Furthermore, the fourth quarter of 2006 was an all-time record quarter for this global market, with $239 billion of transaction volume.

Global debt underwriting also set new all-time records in 2006, increasing 14% to $6.95 trillion from $6.09 trillion in 2005. At the top of this chart again was Citigroup, with $606 billion, followed by #2 JPMorgan with $460 billion. Deutsche Bank captured the #3 ranking with $440 billion in transactions. Early-2000s top players Morgan Stanley and Merrill Lynch now rank #5 and #6, respectively.

As calculated by Freeman & Co. and reported by Thomson Financial, global imputed fees for debt, equity, and equity-related deals continued to surge as well, reaching $42 billion in 2006, up 27% from $33 billion in 2005. Although losing a slight bit of market share, Citigroup remained the top fee earner, with $3.3 billion of calculated imputed fees. Merrill Lynch followed at #2 with $2.7 billion and JPMorgan was #3 with $2.5 billion.

Driven by surges in all markets, global debt, equity, and equity-related issuance reached all-time highs across the board. However, in the U.S., it was Investment Grade Corporate Debt that drove volume, not the equity

Visit the Vault Finance Career Channel at **www.vault.com/finance** – with
insider firm profiles, message boards, the Vault Finance Job Board and more.

VAULT CAREER LIBRARY   **49**

markets. While IG Corporate Debt reached all-time record levels of $919 trillion, an increase of 37% from 2005, issuance in the equity and equity-related markets saw less of an increase, to $208 billion from $169 billion in 2005. Furthermore, in the U.S., the IPO market actually saw a decline in the number of IPOs, down by 19 such issuances. However, IPO proceeds were still up, totaling $44.5 billion in 2006 versus $36.7 in 2005. Goldman retained the #1 IPO market position with 30 deals totaling $7.4 billion, followed by Morgan Stanley with 25 deals totaling $5.3 billion and Citigroup with 22 deals totaling $4.8 billion.

Google: a noun, a verb, an IPO

August 19, 2004 witnessed the most highly anticipated IPO in history (or at least since eBay went public back in 1998). In the second quarter of 2004, the world's top Internet search engine Google Inc. told the SEC it expected to raise as much $2.7 billion through an IPO. No doubt causing investors to drool, Google revealed in its filing that it booked revenues of $389.6 million and net income of $64 million for the first quarter of 2004, up 118 percent and 148 percent, respectively, from the first quarter of 2003. The company also revealed it took in net income of $106.5 million on revenues of $961.9 million for the full year 2003, a rise of 6 percent and 177 percent over 2002 numbers. Scoring the big win of landing lead bookrunner duties on the proposed IPO were Morgan Stanley and Credit Suisse, both of which picked up some hefty fees for their work. Some 30 other investment banking firms also inked deals with Google to co-manage the deal.

Like Google itself, the structure of its initial offering was quite innovative, as the company opted to go public through an auction system. As of June 2004, investors registered with the banks underwriting the offering and indicated the number of shares they wanted to purchase and at what price they were willing to buy them. After that, Google, with the advice of its bankers, determined a price at which all of the bids were sold. Bidders below this price, called a "clearing price," were left out of the action. Ultimately, approximately 19 million shares were offered at $85 a share, raising $1.7 billion for Google and giving the company a market capitalization over $23 billion. In late 2006 and again in early 2007, Google reached an all-time high of $505 per share.

The reasoning behind the auction system as opposed to the traditional offering process, wrote Google co-founders Larry Page and Sergey Brin in the firm's SEC filing, was "to have a fair process" that was "inclusive of both small and large investors." The two also wrote that the firm's "goal is to have a share price that reflects a fair market valuation of Google and that moves rationally based on changes in our business and the stock market."

No doubt, Google has been immensely successful in the past two years. So successful, in fact, that it had a secondary offering of approximately 15 million shares at $295 per share in late 2005, raising over $4 billion. Furthermore, Google was quite active in the M&A market in late 2006, acquiring the consumer media company YouTube for $1.65 billion in a stock transaction. Even more recently, Google has been at it again, announcing its intention to purchase online advertising giant DoubleClick for $3.1 billion.

The banks formerly known as commercial

In 2006, mega-banks with both an investment banking and commercial banking presence continued to prove they are among the elite on Wall Street. For the year, top debt underwriters and traditional lenders Citigroup, JPMorgan Chase, and Bank of America combined to take a 26 percent market share in U.S. equity and equity-relating underwriting. In comparison, Goldman, Morgan Stanley and Merrill, three of the top traditional investment banks, combined for 36 percent of the equity activity in 2006. In recent years, Citigroup and JPMorgan Chase have continually been at the top of many other league tables, thanks in large part to their acquisitions of investment banks and their ability to become one-stop-shops for companies.

These institutions, once thought of as commercial lenders, are now among the elite investment banks on Wall Street as client needs and financial markets have evolved and become more complex. Case in point, as LBO activity has become a major driver of the M&A markets, not surprisingly, those firms that dominate syndicated loan and high-yield bond issuance (typically used to execute an LBO) have also become dominant players in the M&A markets. As the #1 and #2 players in both the syndicated loan and high-yield bond markets, JPMorgan and Citigroup are changing the way the game is played.

Visit the Vault Finance Career Channel at **www.vault.com/finance** – with insider firm profiles, message boards, the Vault Finance Job Board and more.

VAULT CAREER LIBRARY

51

Graduates: Too Hot to Handle

Riding the waves of an exceptionally robust market, employers continue to beef up their hiring efforts. The National Association of Colleges and Employers (NACE) reported the "Best Job Market in Four Years for the Class of 2006," with starting salaries for new college graduates continuing to increase. Specifically, in the area of "business disciplines," salary increases have been seen "across the board" for both accounting graduates as well as business administration/management graduates. In 2007, this trend is expected to continue, with "employers expecting to hire 17.4% more college graduates." Indicative of the competition for top talent, business administration majors are seeing significant pay increases this year, up 9.4% from 2006. In its annual undergraduate business school rankings, *BusinessWeek* echoes these statistics; "recruiting of graduates is up" and "salary offers are higher," especially at perennially top-ranked Wharton.

As for MBAs, NACE's recent surveys indicate that employers are targeting to hire 22% more graduates in 2007 than they hired in 2006. This is great news for those pursuing M.B.A. degrees in particular in the South, where a 59% increase is expected. MBA programs Wharton and HBS attained the top spots, respectively, in CNNMoney's ""Top 50 Business Schools for Getting Hired," with graduates expecting to receive six-figure compensation the first year out of an M.B.A. program.

Equity and Debt Offerings

In this chapter, we will take you through the basics of four types of offerings: the IPO, the follow-on equity offering, the bond offering, and the loan offering.

Initial Public Offerings

An initial public offering (IPO) is the process by which a private company transforms itself into a public company. The company offers, for the first time, shares of its equity (ownership) to the investing public. These shares subsequently trade on a public stock exchange like the New York Stock Exchange (NYSE) or the NASDAQ.

The first question you may ask is why a company would want to go public. Many private companies succeed remarkably well as privately owned enterprises. The largest privately-held company in the U.S., Cargill, books more than $65 billion in annual revenue. And until 1999, one of Wall Street's elite investment banks, Goldman Sachs, was a private company. However, for many large or growing private companies, a day of reckoning comes for the owners when they decide to sell a portion of their ownership in their firm to the public.

The primary reason for going through the rigors of an IPO is to raise cash to fund the growth of a company and to increase a company's ability to make acquisitions using stock. For example, industry observers believe that Goldman Sachs' partners wished to at least have available a publicly traded currency (the stock in the company) with which to acquire other financial services firms.

While obtaining growth capital is the main reason for going public, it is not the only reason. Often, the owners of a company may simply wish to cash out either partially or entirely by selling their ownership in the firm through the offering. Thus, the owners will sell shares in the IPO and get cash for their equity in the firm. This is usually the ideal scenario for a venture capital-owned firm. Or, sometimes a company's CEO may own a majority or all of the equity, and will offer a few shares in an IPO in order to diversify his/her net worth or to gain some liquidity.

To return to the example of Goldman Sachs, some felt that another driving force behind the partners' decision to go public was the feeling that financial markets were at their peak, and that they could get a good price for their equity in their firm. It should be noted that going public is not a slam dunk. Firms that are too small, too stagnant, or have poor growth prospects will—in general—fail to find an investment bank (or at least a top-tier investment bank) willing to underwrite their IPOs.

From an investment banking perspective, the IPO process consists of these three major phases: hiring the mangers, due diligence, and marketing.

Step 1: Hiring the managers. The first step for a company wishing to go public is to hire managers for its offering. This choosing of an investment bank is often referred to as a "beauty contest." Typically, this process involves meeting and interviewing investment bankers from different firms, discussing the firm's reasons for going public, and ultimately nailing down a valuation. In making a valuation, I-bankers, through a mix of art and science, pitch to the company wishing to go public what they believe the firm is worth, and therefore how much stock it can realistically sell. Perhaps understandably, companies often choose the bank that predicts the highest valuation during this beauty contest phase instead of the best-qualified manager. Almost all IPO candidates select two or more investment banks to manage the IPO process. The primary manager is known as the "lead manager," while additional banks are known as "co-managers."

Step 2: Due diligence and drafting. Once managers are selected, the second phase of the IPO process begins. For investment bankers on the deal, this phase involves understanding the company's business (called due diligence) and then filing the legal documents as required by the SEC. The SEC legal form used by a company issuing new public securities is called the S-1 (or prospectus) and requires quite a bit of effort to draft. Generally speaking, the S-1 is a document that provides and overview of the issuance and the company. Lawyers, accountants, I-bankers, and of course company management must toil for countless hours together to complete the S-1 in a timely manner. The final step of filing the completed S-1 usually culminates at "the printer" (see sidebar in Chapter 8).

Step 3: Marketing. The third phase of an IPO is the marketing phase. Once the SEC has approved the prospectus, the company embarks on a roadshow to sell the deal. A roadshow involves flying the company's management coast to coast (and often to Europe) to visit institutional investors potentially interested in buying shares in the offering. Typical roadshows last from two to three weeks, and involve meeting literally hundreds of investors, who listen to the company's PowerPoint presentation and ask scrutinizing questions. Insiders say money managers decide whether or not to invest millions of dollars in a company within just a few minutes of a roadshow presentation.

Step 4: The marketing phase ends abruptly with the placement and final "pricing" of the stock, which results in a new security trading in the market. Investment banks earn fees by taking a percentage commission (called the "underwriting discount," usually around 7-8 percent for an IPO) on the proceeds of the offering. Successful IPOs will trade up on their first day (increase in share price). If the offering is in high demand from investors, underwriters will usually exercise an overallotment option, also known as a "Greenshoe" option, which allows them to sell up to 15% more of the IPO in the market. Young public companies that miss their numbers are dealt with harshly by institutional investors, who not only sell the stock, causing it to drop precipitously, but also quickly lose confidence in the management team.

Follow-on Offerings of Stock

A company that is already publicly traded will sometimes sell stock to the public again. This type of offering is called a follow-on offering, or a secondary offering. As mentioned earlier in the Google example, only a year after its initial IPO, Google was able to capitalize on an increased share price by issuing new shares in a secondary offering. One reason for a follow-on offering is the same as a major reason for the initial offering: a company may be growing rapidly, either by making acquisitions or by internal growth, and may simply require additional capital. Google executed its secondary offering for many of these reasons.

Another reason that a company would issue a follow-on offering is similar to the cashing out scenario in the IPO. In a secondary offering, a large existing shareholder (usually the largest shareholder, say, the CEO or founder) may wish to sell a large block of stock in one fell swoop. Often times this must be done through an additional offering (rather than through a simple sale on the stock market through a broker), because a company may have shareholders with "unregistered" stock who wish to sell large blocks of their shares. By SEC decree, all stock must first be registered by filing an S-1 or similar document before it can trade on a public stock

Visit the Vault Finance Career Channel at **www.vault.com/finance** – with
insider firm profiles, message boards, the Vault Finance Job Board and more.

VAULT CAREER LIBRARY

55

exchange. Thus, pre-IPO shareholders who do not sell shares in the initial offering hold what is called unregistered stock, and are restricted from selling large blocks unless the company registers them. The equity owners who hold the shares sold in an offering, whether it is an IPO or a follow-on, are called the "selling shareholders."

An Example of a Follow-on Offering:
"New" and "Old" Shares

There are two types of shares that are sold in secondary offerings. When a company requires additional growth capital, it sells "new" shares to the public. When an existing shareholder wishes to sell a huge block of stock, "old" shares are sold to the public. Follow-on offerings often include both types of shares.

Let's look at an example. Suppose Acme Company wished to raise $100 million to fund certain growth prospects. Suppose that at the same time, its biggest shareholder, a venture capital firm, was looking to "cash out," or sell its stock.

Assume the firm already had 100 million shares of stock trading in the market. Let's also say that Acme's stock price traded most recently at $10 per share. The current market value of the firm's equity is:

$10 x 100,000,000 shares = $1,000,000,000 ($1 billion)

Say XYZ Venture Capitalists owned 10 million shares (comprising 10 percent of the firm's equity). They want to sell all of their equity in the firm, or the entire 10 million shares. And to raise $100 million of new capital, Acme would have to sell 10 million additional (or new) shares of stock to the public. These shares would be newly created during the offering process. In fact, the prospectus for the follow-on, usually called an S-2 or S-3 (as opposed to the S-1 for the IPO), legally "registers" the stock with the SEC, authorizing the sale of stock to investors.

The total size of the deal would thus need to be 20 million shares, 10 million of which are "new" and 10 million of which are coming from the selling shareholders, the VC firm. Interestingly, because of the additional shares and what is called "dilution of earnings" or "dilution of

EPS," stock prices typically trade down upon a follow-on offering announcement. (Of course, this only happens if the stock to be issued in the deal is "new" stock.)

After this secondary offering is completed, Acme would have 110 million shares outstanding, and its market value would be $1.1 billion if the stock remains at $10 per share. And, the shares sold by XYZ Venture Capitalists will now be in the hands of new investors in the form of freely tradable securities.

Market reaction. What happens when a company announces a secondary offering indicates the market's tolerance for additional equity. Because more shares of stock "dilute" the old shareholders and subsequently "dumps" shares of stock for sale on the market, the stock price usually drops on the announcement of a follow-on offering. Dilution occurs because earnings per share (EPS) in the future will decline, simply based on the fact that more shares will exist post-deal. And since EPS drives stock prices, the share price generally drops.

The process. The follow-on offering process differs little from that of an IPO, and actually is far less complicated. Since underwriters have already represented the company in an IPO, a company often chooses the same managers, thus making the hiring the manager or beauty contest phase much simpler. Also, no real valuation work is required (the market now values the firm's stock), a prospectus has already been written, and a roadshow presentation already prepared. Modifications to the prospectus and the roadshow demand the most time in a follow-on offering, but still can usually be completed with a fraction of the effort required for an initial offering.

Bond Offerings

When a company requires capital, it sometimes chooses to issue public debt instead of equity. According to Thomson Financial, in 2006 in the U.S., there were $919 billion of investment grade corporate bonds issued and $187 billion of high-yield corporate bonds. Generally, a firm undergoing a public bond deal will already have stock trading in the market.

However, it is not uncommon for a financial sponsor to acquire a publicly-traded firm via an LBO (whereby a firm is now "private") and later IPO the firm again. In this situation, the company could have bonds outstanding from its LBO transaction.

The reasons for issuing bonds rather than stock are various. Perhaps the stock price of the issuer is down, and thus a bond issue is a better alternative. Or perhaps the firm does not wish to dilute its existing shareholders by issuing more equity. Or perhaps a company is quite profitable and wants the tax deduction from paying bond interest, while issuing stock offers no tax deduction. These are all valid reasons for issuing bonds rather than equity. Sometimes in down markets, investor appetite for public offerings dwindles to the point where an equity deal just could not get done (investors would not buy the issue).

The bond offering process resembles the IPO process. The primary difference lies in: (1) the focus of the prospectus (a prospectus for a bond offering will emphasize the company's stability and steady cash flow, whereas a stock prospectus will usually play up the company's growth and expansion opportunities), and (2) the importance of the bond's credit rating (the company will want to obtain a favorable credit rating from a debt rating agency like S&P or Moody's, with the help of the "credit department" of the investment bank issuing the bond; the bank's credit department will negotiate with the rating agencies to obtain the best possible rating). As covered in Chapter 5, the better the credit rating—and therefore, the safer the bonds—the lower the interest rate the company must pay on the bonds to entice investors to buy the issue. Clearly, a firm issuing debt will want to have the highest possible bond rating, and hence pay a lower interest rate.

As with stock offerings, investment banks earn underwriting fees on bond offerings in the form of an underwriting discount on the proceeds of the offering. The percentage fee for bond underwriting tends to be lower than for stock underwriting. For more detail on your role as an investment banker in stock and bond offerings, see Chapter 8.

Loan Offerings

Loan offerings are very similar to bond offerings. The major difference between a loan offering and either a bond or an equity offering is that a loan offering is a private process. As the loan is a private security, investors are given private information, such as forward-looking financials, and are restricted from investing in the same company in other public markets. To get around this distinction, many institutional investors will request public-only information, so that they might play in any market they desire.

The issuance process for a syndicated loan is very similar to the bond offering process. Much like the bond, the loan is rated by the credit agencies, an offering memorandum is prepared (similar to a prospectus), and investors are asked to "commit" to the transaction. Unlike a bond offering, a loan offering generally does not involve a roadshow process. Rather, a Lenders' Presentation is prepared and held at one specific location, attended by all invited investors. Another subtle difference in loan offerings is that they are not always underwritten. Often they are arranged on a best-efforts basis, where a certain level of funding isn't necessarily guaranteed. For more information about the differences in the issuance of loans versus bonds, refer to the Vault Career Guide to Leveraged Finance.

Visit the Vault Finance Career Channel at **www.vault.com/finance** — with insider firm profiles, message boards, the Vault Finance Job Board and more.

V/\ULT CAREER LIBRARY

59

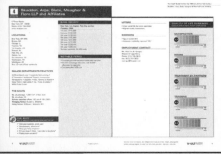

M&A, Private Placements, and Reorgs

CHAPTER 7

Mergers & Acquisitions

Mergers & AcquisitionsIn the 1980s, hostile takeovers and LBO acquisitions were all the rage. Companies sought to acquire others through aggressive stock purchases and cared little about the target company's concerns. The 1990s were the decade of friendly mergers, dominated by a few sectors of the economy. Mergers in the telecommunications, financial services, and technology industries were commanding headlines, as these sectors went through dramatic change, both regulatory and financial. But giant mergers were occurring in virtually every industry (witness one of the biggest of them all, the merger between Exxon and Mobil). Except for short periods of market volatility, M&A (mergers and acquisitions) business was brisk in the 1990s, as demands to go global, to keep pace with the competition, and to expand earnings by any possible means were foremost in the minds of CEOs.

At the beginning of the millennium, however, the M&A slowed. In 2002, the market hit bottom, decreasing in total volume by 40 percent. But in 2003 M&A started its long comeback, as worldwide volume climbed 14 percent versus 2002. This upward trend culminated with global M&A activity setting record highs, at $3.8 trillion, in 2006. Driving this record-setting volume is the return to prominence of LBO and financial sponsor-related activity, comprising 20% of global M&A volume. Indeed, from all aspects, 2006 was a banner year for the global M&A markets.

When a public company acquires another public company, the target company's stock often rises while the acquiring company's stock often declines. Why? One must realize that existing shareholders must be convinced to sell their stock. Few shareholders are willing to sell their stock to an acquirer without first being paid a premium on the current stock price. In addition, shareholders must also capture a takeover premium to relinquish control over the stock. The large shareholders of the target company typically demand such an extraction. (Usually once a takeover is announced, the "arbs" or arbitragers, buy up shares on the open market and drive up the share price to near the proposed takeover price.)

M&A transactions can be roughly divided into either mergers or acquisitions. These terms are often used interchangeably in the press, and the actual legal difference between the two involves arcana of accounting procedures, but we can still draw a rough difference between the two.

Acquisition – When a larger company takes over another (smaller firm) and clearly becomes the new owner, the purchase is typically called an acquisition on Wall Street. Typically, the target company ceases to exist post-transaction (from a legal corporation point of view) and the acquiring corporation swallows the business. The stock of the acquiring company continues to be traded.

Merger – A merger occurs when two companies, often roughly of the same size, combine to create a new company. Such a situation is often called a "merger of equals." Both companies' stocks are tendered (or given up), and new company stock is issued in its place. For example, both Chrysler and Daimler-Benz ceased to exist when their firms merged, and a new combined company, DaimlerChrysler was created.

M&A advisory services

For an I-bank, M&A advising is highly profitable, and there are many possibilities for types of transactions. Perhaps a small private company's owner/manager wishes to sell out for cash and retire. Or perhaps a big public firm aims to buy a competitor through a stock swap. Whatever the case, M&A advisors come directly from the corporate finance departments of investment banks. Unlike public offerings, merger transactions do not directly involve salespeople, traders or research analysts, although research analysts in particular can play an important role in "blessing" the merger. In particular, M&A advisory falls onto the laps of M&A specialists and fits into one of either two buckets: seller representation or buyer representation (also called **target representation** and **acquirer representation**).

Representing the target

An I-bank that represents a potential seller has a much greater likelihood of completing a transaction (and therefore being paid) than an I-bank that represents a potential acquirer. Also known as sell-side work, this type of advisory assignment is generated by a company that approaches an investment bank (also an investment bank may also make the initial approach and "pitch" the idea of the company being sold or merged) and asks the bank to find a buyer of either the entire company or a division. Often, sell-side representation comes when a company asks an investment bank to help it sell a division, plant or subsidiary operation.

Generally speaking, the work involved in finding a buyer includes writing a Selling Memorandum and then contacting potential strategic or financial buyers of the client. If the client hopes to sell a semiconductor plant, for instance, the I-bankers will contact firms in that industry, as well as buyout firms that focus on purchasing technology or high-tech manufacturing operations. In the case of many LBO transactions, a sell-side firm might even hold an "auction" in which it will accept bids for the company, in order to get the seller the best price possible for its property.

Buyout Firms and LBOs

Buyout firms, which are also called financial sponsors, acquire companies, either private or public. To complete an LBO, the financial sponsor invests some of its own cash, while borrowing other cash in the form of loans and bonds. (As a rule of thumb, a financial sponsor will seek to invest 25% of the purchase price from its own pocket, with 75% coming from debt). These buyout firms (also called LBO firms) implement a management team they trust, improve sales and profits, and ultimately seek an exit strategy (usually a sale or IPO) for their investment within a few years. These firms are driven to achieve a high return on investment (ROI), and focus their efforts toward streamlining the acquired business and preparing the company for a future IPO or sale. It is quite common that a buyout firm will be the selling shareholder in an IPO or follow-on offering.

There are a number of major financial sponsors that have raised billions of dollars each for purchasing companies. The most notable financial sponsors include Kohlberg Kravis Roberts, Texas Pacific Group, J. P. Morgan Partners, Blackstone, Thomas H. Lee, Bain Capital, Carlyle Group, Madison Dearborn, Hicks Muse Tate & Furst, DLJ Merchant Banking, Goldman Sachs Capital Partners, and Warburg Pincus. Currently, of this major group, it has been estimated that over $200 billion exists in "dry powder" (cash that has yet to be invested) alone, which could represent nearly $1 trillion of LBO volume in the very near future. In 2006, new records were set with estimated $230 billion of LBO activity, nearly doubling 2005's $130 billion. Yet with so much money left to invest, it appears the best is yet to come.

With so much money chasing these private companies, it comes as little surprise that some of the largest LBOs of all time were executed in 2006. The largest of 2006 (now the second-largest LBO of all time), Equity Office Products, was purchased by Blackstone for $33 billion, and the second-largest of 2006, HCA, by a consortium of investors for

Visit the Vault Finance Career Channel at **www.vault.com/finance** – with insider firm profiles, message boards, the Vault Finance Job Board and more.

VAULT CAREER LIBRARY

63

$32 billion. However, 2007 has only proceeded in this vein of mega-LBOs with the largest LBO of all time, the $45 billion buyout of TXU by KKR and TPG. The most notable LBO (and arguably the largest, due to inflation) remains the 1987 purchase of RJR Nabisco by KKR for $31 billion.

Representing the acquirer

In advising sellers, the I-bank's work is complete once another party purchases the business up for sale, i.e., once another party buys your client's company or division or assets. Buy-side work is an entirely different animal. The advisory work itself is straightforward: the investment bank contacts the firm their client wishes to purchase, attempts to structure a palatable offer for all parties, and makes the deal a reality. (Again, the initial contact may be from the acquiring company. Or the investment bank may "pitch" the idea of an acquisition of Company X to the acquiring company.) However, most of these proposals do not work out; few firms or owners are readily willing to sell their business. And because the I-banks primarily collect fees based on completed transactions, their work often goes unpaid. However, this doesn't stop investment banks from dreaming up new proposals.

Consequently, when advising clients looking to buy a business, an I-bank's work often drags on for months. Often a firm will pay a nonrefundable retainer fee to hire a bank and say, "Find us a target company to buy." These acquisition searches can last for months and produce nothing except associate and analyst fatigue as they repeatedly build merger models and pull all-nighters. Deals that do get done, though, are a boon for the I-bank representing the buyer because of their enormous profitability. Typical fees depend on the size of the deal, but generally fall in the one-two percent range. For a $100 million deal, an investment bank takes home $1-2 million. Not bad for a few months' work.

Private Placements

A **private placement**, which involves the selling of debt or equity to private investors, resembles both a public offering and a merger. A private placement differs little from a public offering aside from the fact that a private placement involves a firm selling stock or equity to private investors rather than to public investors. In this sense, it is very similar to a loan offering. Also, a typical private placement deal is smaller than a public transaction. Despite these differences, the primary reason for a private placement—to raise capital—is fundamentally the same as a public offering. To give a sense of the size of the market, the debt portion of private placements usually hovers around $40 billion of transaction volume, versus the trillions of dollars of volume in the loan and bond markets.

Why private placements?

As mentioned previously, firms wishing to raise capital often discover that they are unable to go public for a number of reasons. The company may not be big enough; the markets may not have an appetite for IPOs, the company may be too young or not ready to be a public company, or the company may simply prefer not to have its stock be publicly traded. Such firms with solidly growing businesses make excellent private placement candidates. Often, firms wishing to go public may be advised by investment bankers to first do a private placement, as they need to gain critical mass or size to justify an IPO.

Private placements, then, are usually the province of smaller companies aiming ultimately to go public. The process of raising private equity or debt changes only slightly from a public deal. One difference is that private placements do not require any securities to be registered with the SEC, nor do they involve a roadshow. In place of the prospectus, I-banks draft a detailed Private Placement Memorandum (PPM for short) which divulges information similar to a prospectus. Instead of a roadshow, companies looking to sell private stock or debt will host potential investors as interest arises, and give presentations detailing how they will be the greatest thing since sliced bread.

Often, one firm will be the sole or lead investor in a private placement. In other words, if a company sells stock through a private placement, often only a handful of institutions will buy the stock offered. Conversely, in an IPO, shares of stock fall into the hands of literally thousands of buyers immediately after the deal is completed.

Visit the Vault Finance Career Channel at **www.vault.com/finance** – with
insider firm profiles, message boards, the Vault Finance Job Board and more.

VAULT CAREER LIBRARY   **65**

The I-bank's role in private placements

The investment banker's work involved in a private placement is quite similar to sell-side M&A representation. The bankers attempt to find a buyer by writing the PPM and then contacting potential strategic or financial buyers of the client.

In the case of equity private placements, however, financial buyers are typically venture capitalists rather than buyout firms, which is an important distinction. A VC firm invests in less than 50 percent of a company's equity, whereas a buyout firm purchases greater than 50 percent and often nearly 100 percent of a company's equity, thereby gaining control of the firm. Note that the same difference applies to private placements on the sell-side. A sale occurs when a firm sells greater than 50 percent of its equity (giving up control), but a private placement occurs usually when less than 50 percent of its equity is sold. Note that in private placements, the company typically offers convertible preferred stock, rather than common stock.

In the case of debt private placements, the buyers tend to be insurance companies and other institutional investors that might be restricted as to the securities they can purchase. However, as with equity private placements, the number of buyers tends to be small, often only a handful.

Debt private placements are structured nearly identically to high yield bonds. Because private placements involve selling equity and debt to a single or limited number of buyers, the investor and the seller (the company) typically negotiate the terms of the deal. Investment bankers function as negotiators for the company, helping to convince the investor of the value of the firm.

Fees involved in private placements work like those in public offerings. Usually they are a fixed percentage of the size of the transaction. (Of course, the fees depend on whether a deal is consummated or not.) A common private placement fee is 5 to 8 percent of the size of the equity/ debt sold.

Financial Restructurings

When a company cannot pay its cash obligations—for example, when it cannot meet its bond interest payments or its payments to other creditors (such as vendors)—it usually must file for bankruptcy court protection from creditors. In this situation, a company can, of course, choose to simply shut down operations and walk away. On the other hand, it can also restructure and remain in business. This restructuring, where the company remains in business, is often referred to as Chapter 11 bankruptcy. Conversely, when the firm is liquidated, this is referred to as Chapter 7 bankruptcy.

What does it mean to restructure? The process can be thought of as twofold: financial restructuring and organizational restructuring. Restructuring from a financial viewpoint involves renegotiating payment terms on debt obligations, issuing new debt, and restructuring payables to vendors.

Bankers provide guidance to the restructuring firm by recommending the sale of assets, the issuing of special securities such as convertible stock, bonds, or loans or even working with M&A bankers to sell the company entirely. Often, the restructuring practice at an investment bank works hand-in-hand with a firm's leveraged finance team, as bankrupt companies generally operate with the same characteristics as highly leveraged firms.

From an organizational viewpoint, a restructuring can involve a change in management, strategy and focus. I-bankers with expertise in "reorgs" can facilitate and ease the transition from bankruptcy to viability. Top tier I-banks specializing in this type of organizational restructuring advisory include Lazard Freres & Co and The Blackstone Group.

From a financial viewpoint, when a company is operating in bankruptcy, it usually must seek the court's approval to execute any major financial transactions, which are done with the help of an I-bank. In order to continue operating, the bankruptcy court will generally allow a restructuring of debt to include DIP (Debtor-in-Possession) loans. Those holding the DIP loans, as well as any other remaining debt, are the firms' creditors. The top providers of these loans include JPMorgan, Citigroup, and GE Capital.

The topic of DIP loans brings about an interesting point. In the event of Chapter 7 liquidation, the most senior creditors are paid out first by the proceeds of the asset sale(s). Usually, once the debt holders have been paid out, there will be little to no value remaining for equity holders. This seniority is one of the many reasons that equity is essentially riskier than debt. The most senior type of debt is "secured," or specifically covered by assets of the company. DIP loans are generally the most senior secured debt, followed by other loans, which are often secured. Bonds are usually senior or junior debt, but not secured. Finally, convertible notes are junior to regular bonds, preferred equity comes next, and common equity brings up the rear.

Visit the Vault Finance Career Channel at **www.vault.com/finance** — with insider firm profiles, message boards, the Vault Finance Job Board and more.

VAULT CAREER LIBRARY   67

Many major firms have been in bankruptcy in the past 10 years. The largest bankruptcy of all-time was Worldcom Inc, which filed for Chapter 11 protection in 2002 with over $100 billion in assets and later exited bankruptcy in 2003 under the name MCI. It's likely that the most notable bankruptcy of all time was Enron, which declared in December 2001. A number of other examples come from an industry that is constantly wrestling with bankruptcy, the airlines. Specifically, United Airlines operated for over 3 years in bankruptcy, exiting in July 2006. Other major airlines that have previously or are currently in bankruptcy include Delta Air Lines, Northwest Airlines, and US Airways. Aside from the airlines, bankruptcy stretches to many other household names including Eddie Bauer, Texaco, and even Interstate Bakeries, which owns Wonder Bread, Twinkies, and Hostess brands.

Although bankrupt companies are generally very risky investments, there stands to be a large reward if they are able to exit, or even improve their financial performance. Many institutional investors have dedicated "distressed debt" operations that seek to invest primarily in bankrupt and other struggling firms. A few well-known hedge funds that invest in distressed debt securities include Cerberus Capital, Highland Capital, and Oaktree Capital Management.

Fees in restructuring work

Typical investment banking fees in a restructuring depend on what new securities are issued post-bankruptcy and whether the company is sold,. However, the fees generally include a retainer fee paid upfront to the investment bank. When a bank represents a bankrupt company, the brunt of the work is focused on analyzing and recommending financing alternatives. Thus, the fee structure resembles that of a private placement. How does the work differ from that of a private placement? I-bankers not only work in securing financing, but may assist in building projections for the client (which serve to illustrate to potential financiers what the firm's prospects may be), in renegotiating credit terms with lenders working with the company's lawyers to navigate through the bankruptcy court process, and in helping to re-establish the business as a going concern.

Because a firm in bankruptcy already has substantial cash flow problems, investment banks often charge minimal monthly retainers, hoping to cash in on the spread from issuing new securities or selling the company. Like other offerings, this can be a highly lucrative and steady business.

The Current Restructuring Market

Right now, there seem to be very few companies declaring bankruptcy, which is measured by the "default rate." According to the SEC, there currently exists one of the lowest default rates in credit history. This can be primarily traced to an overall healthy economy and record-low interest rates. However, as the credit cycle tends to ebb and flow, it is expected that sooner or later, many more firms will be declaring bankruptcy, which will translate into increased I-banking restructuring activity.

Visit the Vault Finance Career Channel at **www.vault.com/finance** — with
insider firm profiles, message boards, the Vault Finance Job Board and more.

V/\ULT CAREER LIBRARY   69

ON THE JOB

Corporate Finance

CHAPTER 8

Stuffy bankers?

The stereotype of the corporate finance department is stuffy, arrogant (white and male) MBAs who frequent golf courses and talk on cell-phones nonstop. While this is increasingly less true, corporate finance remains the most white-shoe department in the typical investment bank. The atmosphere in corporate finance is, unlike that in sales and trading, often quiet and reserved. Junior bankers sit separated by cubicles, quietly crunching numbers.

Depending on the firm, corporate finance can also be a tough place to work, with unforgiving bankers and expectations through the roof. Although decreasing, stories of analyst abuse run rampant and some bankers come down hard on new analysts simply to scare and intimidate them. The lifestyle for corporate finance professionals can be a killer. In fact, many corporate finance workers find that they literally dedicate their lives to the job. Social life suffers, free time disappears, and stress multiplies. It is not uncommon to find analysts and associates wearing rumpled pants and wrinkled shirts, exhibiting the wear and tear of all-nighters. Fortunately, these long hours pay remarkable dividends in the form of six-figure salaries and huge year-end bonuses.

Personality-wise, bankers tend to be highly intelligent, motivated, and not lacking in confidence. Money is very much a driving motivation for bankers, and many anticipate working for just a few years to earn as much as possible, before finding less demanding work. Analysts and associates tend also to be ambitious, intelligent and pedigreed. If you happen to be going into an analyst or associate position, make sure to check your ego at the door but don't be afraid to ask penetrating questions about deals and what is required of you.

The deal team

Investment bankers generally work in deal teams which, depending on the size of a deal, vary somewhat in makeup. In this chapter we will provide an overview of the roles and lifestyles of the positions in corporate finance, from analyst to managing director. (Often, a person in corporate finance is generally called an I-banker.) Because the titles and roles really do not differ significantly between underwriting to M&A, we have included both in this explanation. In fact, at most smaller firms, underwriting and transaction advisory are not separated, and bankers typically pitch whatever business they can scout out within their industry sector.

The Players

Analysts

Analysts are the grunts of the corporate finance world. They often toil endlessly with little thanks, little pay (when figured on an hourly basis), and barely enough free time to sleep four hours a night. Typically hired directly out of top undergraduate universities, this crop of bright, highly motivated kids does the financial modeling and basic entry-level duties associated with any corporate finance deal.

Modeling every night until 2 a.m. and not having much of a social life proves to be unbearable for many an analyst. Furthermore, when not at the office, analysts can be found feverishly typing on their blackberries. Not surprisingly, after two years, many analysts leave the industry. Unfortunately, many bankers recognize the transient nature of analysts, and work them hard to get the most out of them they can. The unfortunate analyst that screws up or talks back too much may never get quality work, spending his days bored until 11 p.m. waiting for work to come, stressing even more than the busy analyst. These are the analysts that do not get called to work on live transactions, and do menial work or just put together pitchbooks all of the time. The very best analysts often get identified early by top performing MDs and VPs, thus finding themselves staffed on many live transactions.

When it comes to analyst pay, much depends on whether the analyst is in New York or not. In the City, salary often begins for first-year analysts at $55,000 to $70,000 per year, with an annual bonus of approximately $60,000-85,000. While this seems to be quite a lot for a 22-year-old with just an undergrad degree, it's not a great deal if you consider per-hour compensation. Bonuses at this level are also force-ranked, thus identifying and compensating top talent. At most firms, analysts also get dinner every night for free if they work late, and have little time to spend their income, often meaning fat checking and savings accounts and ample fodder to fund business school or law school down the road. At regional firms, pay typically is 20 percent less than that of their New York counterparts. Worth noting, though, is the fact that at regional firms 1) hours are often less, and

2) the cost of living is much lower. Be wary, however, of the small regional firm or branch office of a Wall Street firm that pays at the low end of the scale and still shackles analysts to their cubicles.

Regardless of location, while the salary generally does not improve much for second-year analysts, the bonus will dramatically increase for those second-years who demonstrate high performance. At this level, bonuses depend mostly on an analyst's contribution, attitude, and work ethic, as opposed to the volume of business generated by the bankers with whom he or she works.

Associates

Much like analysts, associates hit the grindstone hard. Working 80- to 100 hour weeks, usually fresh out of top-tier MBA programs, associates stress over pitchbooks and models all night, become experts with financial modeling on Excel, and sometimes shake their heads wondering what the point is. Unlike analysts, however, associates more quickly become involved with clients and, most importantly, are not at the bottom of the totem pole. Associates quickly learn to play quarterback and hand-off menial modeling work and research projects to analysts. However, treatment from vice presidents and managing directors doesn't necessarily improve for associates versus analysts, as bankers sometimes care more about the work getting done, and not about the guy or gal working away all night to complete it.

Usually hailing directly from top business schools (sometimes law schools or other grad schools), associates often possess only a summer's worth of experience in corporate finance, so they must start almost from the beginning. Associates who worked as analysts before grad school have a little more experience under their belts. The overall level of business awareness and knowledge a bright MBA has, however, makes a tremendous difference, and associates quickly earn the luxury of more complicated work, client contact, and bigger bonuses.

Associates are at least much better paid than analysts. A $95,000 to $100,000 salary generally starts them off, and usually bonuses hit $35,000-$55,000+ in the first six months. (At most firms, associates start in August and get their first prorated bonus in January.) Newly minted MBAs cash in on signing bonuses and forgivable loans as well, especially on Wall Street. These can amount to another $35,000 to $55,000, depending on the firm, providing total first-year compensation over $200,000 for top firms. Associates beyond their first year begin to rake it in, earning $250,000 to

Visit the Vault Finance Career Channel at **www.vault.com/finance** – with insider firm profiles, message boards, the Vault Finance Job Board and more.

VAULT CAREER LIBRARY

75

$500,000 and up per year, depending on the firm's profitability and other factors.

Vice Presidents

Upon attaining the position of vice president (at most firms, after four or five years as associates), those in corporate finance enter the realm of real bankers. The lifestyle becomes more manageable once the associate moves up to VP. On the plus side, weekends sometimes free up, all-nighters drop off, and the general level of responsibility increases—VPs are the ones telling associates and analysts to stay late on Friday nights. In the office, VPs manage the financial modeling/pitchbook production process in the

Corporate Finance

office. On the negative side, the wear and tear of traveling that accompanies VP-level banker responsibilities can be difficult. As a VP, one begins to handle client relationships, and thus spends much more time on the road than analysts or associates. As a VP, you can look forward to being on the road at least two to four days per week, usually visiting current and potential clients. Don't forget about closing dinners (to celebrate completed deals), industry conferences (to drum up potential business and build a solid network within their industry), and, of course, roadshows. VPs are perfect candidates to baby-sit company management on roadshows.

Directors/Managing Directors

Directors and managing directors (MDs) are the major players in corporate finance. Typically, MDs set their own hours, deal with clients at the highest level, and disappear whenever a drafting session takes place, leaving this grueling work to others. (We will examine these drafting sessions in depth later.) MDs mostly develop and cultivate relationships with various companies in order to generate corporate finance business for the firm. At this point in a banker's career, the job completes the transition from managing a process to managing a relationship. MDs typically focus on one industry, develop relationships among management teams of companies in the industry, and visit these companies pitching ideas on a regular basis. These visits are aptly called sales calls.

Pay scales

The formula for paying bankers varies dramatically from firm to firm. Some adhere to rigid formulas based on how much business a banker brought in, while others pay based on a subjective allocation of corporate finance profits. No matter how compensation is structured, however, when business is slow, bonuses taper off rapidly. For most bankers, typical salaries may range from $150,000 to $200,000 per year, but bonuses can be significantly greater. Total packages for VPs on Wall Street often hit over $500,000 level in the first year—and pay can skyrocket from there.

Top bankers at the MD level might be pulling in bonuses of up to $2-3 million or more a year, with group and department heads even getting signed to long-term contracts. But slow markets (and hence slow business) can cut that number dramatically. It is important to realize that for the most part, MDs act as relationship managers, and are essentially paid on commission. For top performers, compensation can be almost inconceivable.

The Role of the Players

What do corporate finance professionals actually do on a day-to-day basis to underwrite an offering? The process, though not simple, can easily be broken up into the same three phases that we described previously. We will illustrate the role of the bankers by walking through the IPO process in more detail. Note that other types of equity or debt offerings closely mirror the IPO process.

Hiring the managers

This phase in the process can vary in length substantially, lasting for many months or just a few short weeks. The length of the hiring phase depends on how many I-banks the company wishes to meet, when they want to go public, and how market conditions fare. Remember that two or more investment banks are usually tapped to manage a single equity or debt deal, complicating the hiring decisions that companies face.

MDs and sales calls

Often when a large IPO candidate is preparing for an offering, word gets out on the Street that the company is looking to go public. MDs all over Wall Street scramble to create pitchbooks (see sidebar on next page) and set up meetings called "pitches" in order to convince the company to hire them as the lead manager. I-bankers who have previously established a good relationship with the company have a distinct advantage. What is surprising

Visit the Vault Finance Career Channel at **www.vault.com/finance** – with insider firm profiles, message boards, the Vault Finance Job Board and more.

VAULT CAREER LIBRARY

77

to many people unfamiliar with I-banking is that MDs are essentially traveling salespeople who pay visits to the CEOs and CFOs of companies, with the goal of building investment banking relationships.

Typically, MDs meet informally with the company several times. In an initial meeting with a firm's management, the MD will have an analyst and an associate put together a general pitchbook, which is left with the company to illustrate the I-bank's capabilities.

Once an MD knows a company plans to go public, he or she will first discuss the IPO with the company's top management and gather data regarding past financial performance and future expected results. This data, farmed out to a VP or associate and crucial to the valuation, is then used in the preparation of the pitchbook.

A Word About Pitchbooks

Pitchbooks come in two flavors: the general pitchbook and the deal-specific pitchbook. Bankers use the general pitchbook to guide their introductions and presentations during sales calls. These pitchbooks contain general information and include a wide variety of selling points bankers make to potential clients. Usually, general pitchbooks include an overview of the I-bank and detail its specific capabilities in research, corporate finance, sales and trading.

The second flavor of pitchbooks is the deal-specific pitch. While a general pitchbook does not differ much from deal to deal, bankers prepare offering pitchbooks specifically for the transactions (for example, an IPO or proposed sale of the company) they are proposing to a company's top managers. Deal-specific pitchbooks are highly customized and usually require analyst or associate all-nighters to put together (although MDs, VPs, associates, and analysts all work closely together to create the book). The most difficult aspect to creating this type of pitchbook is the financial modeling involved. In an IPO pitchbook, valuations, comparable company analyses, and industry analyses are but a few of the many specific topics covered in detail.

Apart from the numbers, these pitchbooks also include the bank's customized selling points. The most common of these include:

- The bank's reputation, which can lend the offering an aura of respectability

- The performance of other IPOs or similar offerings managed by the bank

- The prominence of a bank's research analyst in the industry, which can tacitly guarantee that the new public stock will receive favorable coverage by a listened-to stock expert

- The bank's expertise as an underwriter in the industry, including its ranking in the "league tables" (rankings of investment banks based on their volume of offerings handled in a given category)

Pitchbook preparation

After substantial effort and probably a few all-nighters on the part of analysts and associates, the deal-specific pitchbook is complete. The most important piece of information in this kind of pitchbook is the valuation of the company going public. Prior to its initial public offering, a company has no public equity and therefore no clear market value of common stock. So, the investment bankers, through a mix of financial and industry expertise, including analysis of comparable public companies, develop a suitable offering size range and hence a marketable valuation range for the company. Of course, the higher the valuation, the happier the potential client. At the same time, though, I-bankers must not be too aggressive in their valuation – if the market does not support the valuation and the IPO fails, the bank loses credibility.

The pitch

While analysts and associates are the members of the **deal team** who spend the most time working on the pitchbook, the MD is the one who actually visits the company with the books under his or her arm to make the pitch, perhaps with a VP. The pitchbook serves as a guide for the presentation (led by the MD) to the company. This presentation generally concludes with the valuation. Companies invite many I-banks to present their pitches at separate meetings. These multiple rounds of presentations comprise what is often called the beauty contest or beauty pageant.

The pitch comes from the managing director in charge of the deal. The MD's supporting cast typically consists of a VP from corporate finance, as well as the research analyst who will cover the company's stock once the IPO is complete. For especially important pitches, an I-bank will send other top representatives from either its corporate finance, research or syndicate

Visit the Vault Finance Career Channel at **www.vault.com/finance** – with insider firm profiles, message boards, the Vault Finance Job Board and more.

VAULT CAREER LIBRARY

79

departments. (We will cover the syndicate and research departments later.) Some companies opt to have their board of directors sit in on the pitch – the MD might face the added pressure of tough questions from the board during the presentation.

Selecting the managers

After a company has seen all of the pitches in a beauty contest, it selects one firm as the lead manager, while some of the other firms are chosen as the co-managers. The number of firms chosen to manage a deal runs the gamut. Sometimes a firm will sole manage a deal, and sometimes, especially on large global deals, four to six firms might be selected as managers. An average-sized offering will generally have three to four managers underwriting the offering—one lead manager and two or three co-managers. When the prospectus or offering memorandum is actually printed, the firm on the far-left (referred to as "lead-left") is the one running the deal. From here, the firms are organized from left to right, in order of importance.

Due diligence and drafting

Organizational meeting

Once the I-bank has been selected as a manager in the IPO, the next step is an organizational meeting at the company's headquarters. All parties in the working group involved in the deal meet for the first time, shake hands and get down to business. The attendees and their roles are summarized in the table below.

Group	Typical Participants
The Company	Management, namely the CEO and CFO, division heads, and heads of major departments or lines of business.
The Company's lawyers	Partner plus one associate.
The Company's accountants	Partner, plus one or two associates.
The lead manager	I-banking team, with up to four corporate finance professionals. A research analyst may come for due diligence meetings.
The co-manager(s), or I-bank(s) selected behind the lead	I-banking team with typically two or three members instead of four.

Group	Typical Participants
Underwriters' counsel, or the lawyers representing the managers	Partner plus one associate.

At the initial organizational meeting, the MD from the lead manager guides and moderates the meeting. Details discussed at the meeting include the exact size of the offering, the timetable for completing the deal, and other concerns the group may have. Usually a two- or three-month schedule is established as a beacon toward the completion of the offering. A sheet is distributed so all parties can list home, office, and cell phone numbers. Often, the organizational meeting wraps up in an hour or two and leads directly to due diligence.

Due diligence

Due diligence involves studying the company going public in as much detail as possible. Much of this process involves interviewing senior management at the firm. Due diligence usually entails a plant tour (if relevant), and explanations of the company's business, how the company operates, how management plans to grow the company, and how the company will perform over the next few quarters. Often the investment bank will work with the company to setup a "data room" where important company information is housed for use by the investment bank in its diligence process. Historically, this used to be a physical room at the company, but now is generally an online site.

As with the organizational meeting, the moderator and lead questioner throughout the due diligence sessions is the senior banker in attendance from the lead manager. Research analysts from the I-banks attend the due diligence meetings during the IPO process in order to probe the business, ask tough questions and generally better understand how to project the company's financials. While bankers tend to focus on the relevant operational, financial, and strategic issues at the firm, lawyers involved in the deal explore mostly legal issues, such as pending litigation.

Drafting the prospectus

Once due diligence wraps up, the IPO process moves quickly into the drafting stage. Drafting refers to the process by which the working group writes the S-1 registration statement, or prospectus. This prospectus is the legal document used to shop the offering to potential investors.

Generally, the client company's lawyers ("issuer's counsel") compile the first draft of the prospectus, but thereafter the drafting process includes the entire working group. Unfortunately, writing by committee means a multitude of style clashes, disagreements, and tangential discussions, but the end result usually is a prospectus that most team members can live with. On average, the drafting stage takes anywhere from four to seven drafting sessions, spread over a six- to 10-week period. Initially, all of the top corporate finance representatives from each of the managers attend, but these meetings thin out to fewer and fewer members as they continue. The lead manager will always have at least a VP to represent the firm, but co-managers often settle on VPs, associates, and sometimes even analysts to represent their firms.

Drafting sessions are initially exciting to attend as an analyst or associate, as they offer client exposure, learning about a business, and getting out of the office. However, these sessions can quickly grow tiring and annoying. Final drafting sessions at the printer can mean more all-nighters, as the group scrambles to finish the prospectus in order to file on time with the SEC.

Going to the Printer

When a prospectus is near completion, lawyers, bankers and the company's senior management all go to the printer, which, as one insider says, is "sort of like going to a country club prison." These 24-hour financial printers (the largest chains are Bowne and Donnelley), where prospectuses are actually printed, are equipped with showers, all the food you can eat, and other amenities to accommodate locked-in-until-you're-done sessions.

Printers are employed by companies to print and distribute prospectuses. A typical public deal requires anywhere from 10,000 to 20,000 copies of the preliminary prospectus (called the red herring or red) and 5,000 to 10,000 copies of the final prospectus. Printers receive the final edited version from the working group, literally print the thousands of copies in-house and then mail them to potential investors in a deal. (The list of investors comes from the managers.) Printers also file the document electronically with the SEC via the "EDGAR" system. As the last meeting before the prospectus is completed, printer meetings can last anywhere from a day to a week or even more. Why is this significant? Because printers are extraordinarily expensive and companies are eager to move onto the next phase of the deal. This amounts to loads of pressure on the working group to finish the prospectus.

For those in the working group, perfecting the prospectus means wrangling over commas, legal language, and grammar until the document is error-free. Nothing is allowed to interrupt a printer meeting, meaning one or two all-nighters in a row is not unheard of for working groups.

On the plus side, printers stock anything and everything that a person could want to eat or drink. The best restaurants cater to printers, and M&M's always seem to appear on the table just when you want a handful. And food isn't all: Many printers have pool tables and stocked bars for those half-hour breaks at 2:00 a.m. Needless to say, an abundance of coffee and fattening food keeps the group going during late hours.

Marketing

Designing marketing material

Once a deal is filed with the SEC, the prospectus (or S-1) becomes public domain. The information and details of the upcoming IPO are publicly known. After the SEC approves the prospectus, the printer spits out thousands of copies, which are mailed to literally the entire universe of potential institutional investors.

In the meantime, the MD and VP of the lead manager work closely with the CEO and CFO of the company to develop a roadshow presentation, which consists of essentially 20 to 40 slides for use during meetings with investors. Junior team members in corporate finance help edit the roadshow slides and begin working on other marketing documents. For example, associates and analysts develop a summary re-hash of the prospectus in a brief "selling memo," which contains key selling points for salespeople to use in pitching the offering to clients and is distributed to the bank's salesforce.

The roadshow (babysitting)

The actual roadshow begins soon after the reds are printed. The preliminary prospectus, called a red herring or red, helps salespeople and investors alike

Going Public

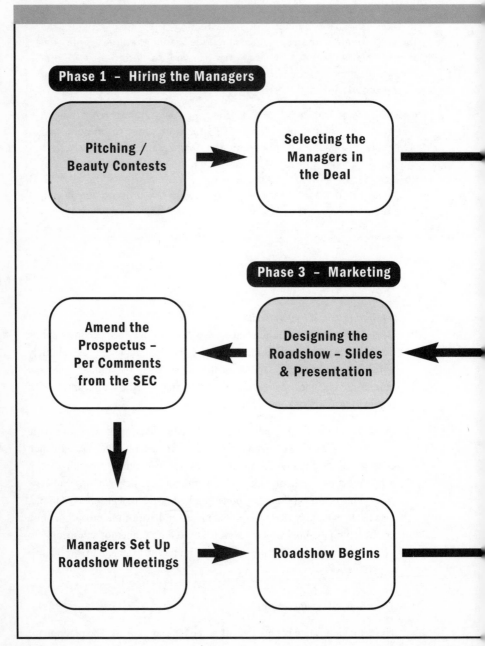

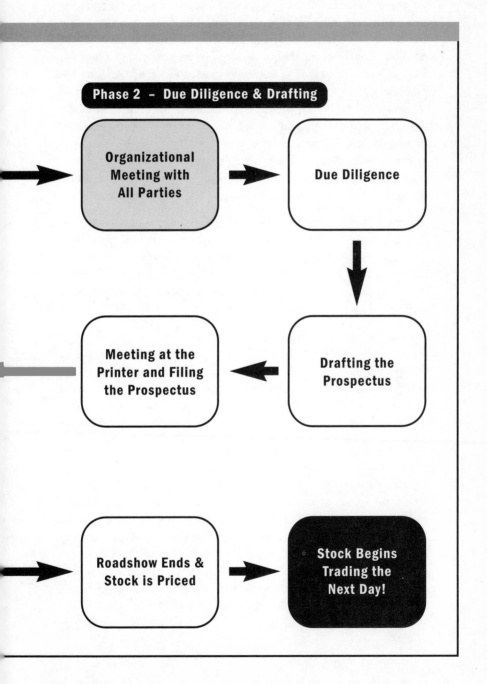

Visit the Vault Finance Career Channel at **www.vault.com/finance** – with
insider firm profiles, message boards, the Vault Finance Job Board and more.

V/\ULT CAREER LIBRARY

85

understand the IPO candidate's business, historical financial performance, growth opportunities, and risk factors. Using the prospectus and the selling memo as references, the salespeople of the investment banks managing the deal contact the institutional investors they cover and set up roadshow meetings. The syndicate department, the facilitators between the salesperson and corporate finance, finalizes the abundance of meetings and communicates the agenda to corporate finance and sales. And, on the roadshow itself, VPs or associates generally escort the company. Despite the seemingly glamorous nature of a roadshow (traveling all over the country in limos and chartered jets with your client, the CEO), the corporate finance professional acts as little more than a babysitter. The most important duties of the junior corporate finance professionals often include making sure luggage gets from point A to point B, ensuring that hotel rooms are booked, and finding the limousine driver at the airport terminal.

After a grueling two to three weeks and literally hundreds of presentations, the roadshow ends and the group flies home for much needed rest. During the roadshow, sales and syndicate departments compile orders for the company's stock and develop what is called "the book.". The book details how investors have responded, how much stock they want (if any), and at what price they are willing to buy into the offering.

The end in sight – pricing the deal

IPO prospectuses list a range of stock prices on the cover (for example, between $16 to $18 per share). This range is preset by the underwriting team before the roadshow and meant to tell investors what the company is worth and hence where it will price. Highly sought-after offerings will price at or even above the top of the range and those in less demand will price at the bottom of the range.

Hot IPOs with tremendous demand end up above the range and often trade up significantly on the first day in the market. The hottest offerings have closed two to three times higher than the initial offering price. Memorable examples include Apple Computer in the 1980s, Boston Chicken in the mid-90s, and Netscape Communications and a slew of Internet stocks in late 1998 through early 2000. The process of going public is summarized graphically on pages 64-65. More recently, though, hot offerings have seen more modest first-day rises. Google's stock, offered to the public in August 2004, only increased 18 percent on its initial day of trading.

Follow-on public offerings and bond offerings

Bond deals and follow-on offerings are less complex in nature than IPOs for many reasons. The biggest reason is that they have an already agreed-upon and approved prospectus from prior publicly filed documents. The language, content, and style of the prospectus usually stay updated year to year, as the company either files for additional offerings or files its annual report (officially called the 10K). Also, the fact that the legal hurdles involved in registering a company's securities have already been leaped makes life significantly easier for everyone involved in a follow-on or bond offering.

If a follow-on offering involves the I-banks that handled a company's IPO (and they often do), the MDs that worked on the deal are already familiar with the company. They may not even have to develop a pitchbook to formally pitch the follow-on if the relationship is sound. Because the banking relationship is usually between individual bankers and individual executives at client companies, bankers can often take clients with them if they switch banks.

Because of their relative simplicity, follow-ons and bond deals quickly jump from the manager-choosing phase to the due diligence and drafting phase, which also progresses more quickly than it would for an IPO. The roadshow proceeds as before, with the company and a corporate finance VP or associate accompanying management to ensure that the logistics work out.

The Typical Week in Corporate Finance

One of the most common questions an interviewee asks is "What is the typical day for an investment banker like?" Truth be told, days spent in investment banking often vary widely, depending on what aspect of a deal you might be working on. But because deals are similar, you might be able to conjure up a typical week in the life of an analyst, associate, vice president, or managing director in corporate finance. We'll start with analysts.

Analysts

For I-banking analysts, it's all about the computer screen. Analysts, especially those in their first year, spend countless hours staring at their computer monitors and working until midnight or all night. Building models, creating "comps," (see sidebar) and editing pitchbooks fills the majority of their time. Many analysts do nothing but put together pitchbooks and models, rarely seeing the light of day. Hard working and talented analysts, however, tend to find their way out of the office and become involved in meetings related to live transactions.

A typical week for an analyst might involve the following:

Monday

Up at 7:30 a.m. Monday morning, the analyst makes it into the office by 9. Mornings often move at a snail's pace, so the analyst builds a set of comparable company analysis (a.k.a. comps, see sidebar) and then updates the latest league table data, which track how many deals I-banks have completed. Lunch is a leisurely forty-five minutes spent with other analysts at a deli a few blocks away. The afternoon includes a conference call with a company considering an IPO, and at 5, a meeting with a VP who drops a big model on the analyst's lap. Dinner is delivered at 8 and paid for by the firm, but this is no great joy – it is going to be a late night because of the model. At midnight, the analyst has reached a stopping point and calls a car service to give him a free ride home.

Tuesday

The next day is similar, but the analyst spends all day working on a pitchbook for a meeting on Wednesday that a banker has set up. Of course, the banker waited until the day before the meeting to tell the analyst about it. After working all night and into the morning, including submitting numerous changes to the 24-hour word processing department, the analyst finally gets home at 5 a.m., which gives him enough time for a two-hour nap, a shower, and a change of clothes.

Wednesday

Unfortunately, there is a scheduled drafting session out of town on Wednesday relating to another transaction, and the flight is at 8 a.m. Having slept only two hours, the analyst reads his draft of the prospectus on the plane, and arrives with a VP at the law firm's office at 11 a.m., armed with some comments to point out to the group. Many hours and coffees later, the VP and analyst get back on the plane, where the analyst falls dead asleep. After the flight touches down, the analyst returns to the office at 8 p.m. – and continues modeling for a few hours. At midnight, the analyst heads home.

Thursday

The analyst is roped into doing another pitchbook, this one for a merger deal. He frantically works to complete a merger model: gathering information, keying in data, and working with an associate looking over his shoulder. By the time he and the associate have finished the analysis, it is 1 a.m.

Friday

Friday is even worse. The merger model is delivered to the hands of the senior VP overseeing the work, but returned covered in red ink. Changes take the better part of the day, and progress is slow. Projections have to be rejiggered, more research found, and new companies added to the list of comps. At 7 p.m. on Friday, the analyst calls his friends to tell them he won't make it out tonight – again. At 11 p.m., he heads home.

Saturday

Even Saturday requires nearly 10 hours of work, but much of the afternoon the analyst waits by the phone to hear from the VP who is looking at the latest version of the models.

Sunday

No rest on Sunday. This day involves checking some numbers, but the afternoon, thankfully, is completely free for some napping and downtime.

The analyst adds up a total of maybe 90 hours this week. It could have been much worse: at some firms, analysts typically work more than 100 hours per week.

Comps, Illustrated

What exactly are **comps**? You may have heard of comps, or comparable company analysis – and the fact that after two years, analysts never want to do comp analysis ever again.

In short, comps summarize financial market measures of similar companies within an industry group. For example, suppose we wanted to compare a software company (our client, Company C, which is considering a sale of the company to other software companies), Companies A and B. Comps usually are many pages long, but often begin with something like the following.

Last 12 Months Data ($ in millions)

Company	Sales	EBITDA	Net Income	EPS	Stock Price
A	2,800	500	200	$ 2.00	$ 75.00
B	900	200	50	$ 0.65	$ 18.00
C	3,000	600	195	$ 1.15	$ 48.75

Valuation Measures

Company	Shares (millions)	Market Value	Net Debt	Enterprise Value
A	100	7,500	1,450	8,950
B	77	1,385	600	1,985
C	170	8,266	190	8,456

Ratios and Multiples

Company	Ent Value/ Revenue	Ent Value/ EBITDA	Price/ Earning
A	3	18	38
B	2	10	28
C	3	14	42

Here we begin to summarize income statement data, including sales and EPS and build up to market valuation measures and, finally, a few ratios. From this illustration, we could interpret the numbers above as: "Our client (Company C) is the biggest firm in terms of sales, has the most cash flow, and the highest P/E ratio. The high P/E ratio makes Company C the most "expensive" stock, trading at 42 times earnings. Note that EBITDA is often used as a proxy for cash flow. (continued...)

Such analyses help bankers interpret how firms are trading in the market, how they compare to their peers, and what valuations seem typical. Comps are useful for valuing companies going public as well as valuing companies that are acquisition targets. Keep in mind that this is a very simplified version of what true comps look like.

A Day in the Life: Analyst, Investment Banking (UBS)

8:00 a.m.: This is a good time to start for first-year analysts; everyone else comes in a half an hour or an hour later.

8:03 a.m.: Upon entering cube/office, check to see if voice mail light is on. If it's Monday, pray to God it's not on, because that means you didn't check it over the weekend and someone might have had work for you to do and wants it in an hour from now (or worse, wanted it yesterday).

8:05 a.m.: Get hot coffee or tea; you'll need it to wake up. Also, out of camaraderie, get one for other analyst guy who didn't go home in the first place. He'll thank you for it, though he probably won't know your name in his state of stupor.

8:10 a.m.: Check e-mail. Receive a bunch of transaction announcements from all over the world, as well as some newsletter relevant to your industry/group sent out by another analyst to everyone. Unless you're into the latest news on, say, regulatory decisions on telecoms or the roofing equipment industry, it's safe to delete and go on with the remainder of e-mails. E-mail might contain information requests by others in the firm, asking for case studies, connections with certain personnel at client firms, etc. As an analyst, you won't know most of this stuff anyway, so hit delete.

8:30 a.m.: Look nervously around the corner to see if associate or director has arrived, so nobody catches you reading a chapter in that novel you've been trying to finish on the weekends and spare morning hours for the past six months.

9:00 a.m.: Office/floor officially running, phones ringing, workday starts. Greet the assistants. Don't call them secretaries. Make sure they like you—so that you can avoid a short-lived career.

9:15 a.m.: After waiting for five minutes for the slow network to load, find your files and continue working on research/modeling—whatever you didn't finish the night before because you knew you still had this morning.

9:17 a.m.: Phone rings. Director/associate calls you for status on the one thing you haven't finished yet. Hold him off until you can finish it and curse yourself for not finishing up last night.

9:30 a.m.: Phone rings again. You know what director/associate is going to say so right off the bat you say, "I'm almost done." Then in between a lot of "oks" you curse your computer for being so slow.

10:00 a.m.: Conference call with deal team, which may include people from other product and industry groups who work in conjunction on a project with you. Managing director is likely to read over material that you were 90 percent responsible for—but only your associate and director know this. Pray nothing's wrong with numbers and grammar.

11:10 a.m.: Too early for lunch but you're already hungry. What to do before lunch? Put together a few public information books ("PIBs"), work on a pitch book or still try to balance your model, which won't happen because you're too hungry to concentrate.

11:15 a.m.: Call up any other analyst buddy in some other group or office and make small talk. He won't have time to talk to you anyway, but it beats having to look at the model again.

12:30 p.m.: You're really hungry but you must print out some files for your associate/director before you leave, so nobody will come around looking for you when they need the printouts. E-mail only if they ask for it. They'll forget it's there anyway.

12:45 p.m.: Lunch across the street or, if you feel rich, pick up food from some fancy sandwich place a few miles away as a sign of your protest to the cafeteria's overpriced salads. Always take cell phone and BlackBerry with you.

1:45 p.m.: Return to work and hope nobody cared that you were gone for an hour. Hope the firm is truly "European" and understands your need for long lunches.

2:00 p.m.: Try not to fall asleep because of the heavy wrap or potatoes you had for lunch. Drink lots of water. Sit down with associate to talk about some preliminary research he needs you to pull from all kinds of sources. He tells you a few other things and leaves you alone. Take notes so as not to forget a single thing. Best excuse later: "I only did what you told me to." This works only if you really did exactly that. Wait for presentations department to turn around a job you sent with the director's changes. He always has some.

3:00 p.m.: New business coming in through another managing director. Your task, should you accept (and you will), is to fill out the first in a long series of forms that will be submitted to one committee after another for review. Essentially, every form looks the same and involves a "company overview." If this is a form for a credit approval committee for a "risky" company, be prepared to write 75 to 100 pages worth of memo, the contents of which are virtually identical with the company's 10-K. But, it has to be in UBS format ,so you can't just pass along the 10-K. You will agonize over the outline and dig through countless sources to extract information and dump it, re-formatted, into your growing file. This will take the rest of the week if your managing director planned ahead. Otherwise, the loan commitment is due in two days and you will not sleep.

4:30 p.m.: It's fair game that anyone, anywhere, anyplace can walk by or call you up during this time for tasks/chores, like putting together a set of trading/transaction comparables, make more PIBs, do extra research, fetch a few industry reports, download files accessible to everyone on the Internet, make printouts, put together working group lists for deal teams on a transaction, etc. Help out other analysts calling for some files or work you've done on something so they don't have to start from scratch on their related project. Sometimes a managing director calls and asks you something you could not possibly know. Sound as smart as possible and then defer the question to your associate.

6:30 p.m.: Order dinner. At UBS, any dinner ordered before this time is not eligible for refund. Adjust stomach and eating habits accordingly from day one, or suffer irritability and lack of concentration going forward. Everyone asks you to put it on your corporate Amex card. Make sure you have enough on your personal bank balance to pay the full amount when the bill is due later, since your refund through the ubiquitous UBS expense system will take a month to process. Run

Visit the Vault Finance Career Channel at **www.vault.com/finance** – with insider firm profiles, message boards, the Vault Finance Job Board and more.

V/\ULT CAREER LIBRARY   93

around with list of who wants what, don't make suggestions, don't write down the wrong thing, and get on with it.

6:35 p.m.: Wait for dinner. (An alternative to waiting might be: A managing director/executive director gives a director a call. The director calls an associate. The associate calls you, and you're evening/week/weekend is ruined because a client wants presentation and model X by the end of next week. The managing director assured the client we'd deliver model X by Monday, "no problem at all." He also said, "While we're at it, we'll also supply Y, Z and A and the reverse of X for two other companies" to further elucidate the issue for the client, who said he really doesn't need all this. But after gentle insistence by the managing director, the client consents, and is glad he went with an ambitious firm such as UBS. After the director gives last instructions to associate or you, then wait for dinner.)

7:45 p.m.: Eat dinner, chat with other analysts about what's up. Take great interest in rumors, gossip and all kinds of BS that would get you fired if you spoke about it outside the conference room you're all huddled in.

8:35 p.m.: Return to work. Call up internal library for some research you don't have access to and hope someone's still there, or it will be a tight morning tomorrow.

10:00 p.m.: Associate leaves, giving you a couple more things to do on way out. "Take your time, no rush," he assures and thanks you for the good job you've been doing in advance. You appreciate his gratitude but would also like to go home at some point.

11:00 p.m.: Discounted cash flow model inputs take very long and the model still doesn't balance. It will be a long night.

2:00 a.m.: You check your e-mail one more time (in fact, you never close it in the first place, as this is the first rule of survival for anyone in investment banking), then you make sure everything is saved, and log out the computer. Call a car and get some sleep.

Associates

With a role similar to analysts, associates are primarily responsible for financial models and pitchbooks. A week for an associate (especially a first-year associate) might resemble closely the scenario painted above, with oversight duties over analysts working on models for the associate. In addition, the associate may be more involved in dealing with the MDs and in checking pitchbooks before they are sent out.

A more experienced associate will sit down more frequently with a VP or MD, going over details of potential deals or discussing numbers. In contrast to analysts, who might work as generalists, associates typically focus on one specific industry. One week for an analyst might include deals for a steel company, a high-tech company, and a restaurant company; an associate will typically focus on an industry like high tech or health care. However, like analysts, associates must work carefully and thoughtfully and put in long hours to gain the respect of their supervisors.

A Day in the Life: Associate, Investment Banking (Goldman Sachs)

8:30 a.m.: Get in. Check e-mail and voice mail.

9:00 a.m.: Breakfast with summer associates "to see how they're doing."

10:00 a.m.: A couple of conference calls with clients that are usually "30-minute phone meetings talking about what I'm planning on presenting to clients next week, and to find out what other topics I should discuss. We basically share ideas."

11:00 a.m.: E-mailing results of conference call meeting to MDs.

11:30 a.m.: Meet with analysts to assign them work. ("I usually give work to full-time analysts and let them run with it. For summer analysts, I'll make sure they're getting a good perspective and are learning. I'll also make sure I'm giving them enough to test them to see if they get it, and have what it takes to be a full-time analyst.)

12:30 p.m.: Lunch. ("About four days a week I grab a sandwich at a deli and eat it at my desk. Sometimes, with a group of people, I eat at

Visit the Vault Finance Career Channel at **www.vault.com/finance** – with insider firm profiles, message boards, the Vault Finance Job Board and more.

VAULT CAREER LIBRARY   95

the cafeteria, which is pretty good. They recently redid the cafeteria. It used to be a dump.")

1:30 p.m.: Conference call with a Goldman MD and a client's CEO about meeting next week.

3:00 p.m.: Prepare reports based on call for meetings next week.

6:30 p.m.: Meet with analysts to dole out work such as research and financial modeling.

7:00 p.m.: Order dinner and eat with a few other people in the office.

8:00 p.m.: Continue on reports for tomorrow's and next week's meetings.

12:00 a.m.: Call car and head home. ("When you leave all depends. On average I leave around midnight, but it's not uncommon to leave after 1 a.m. And sometimes, not often but during slow times, I'll leave as early as 7:30 p.m. or 8:00 p.m.. Third-year associates work between 10 and 20 hours collectively on the weekends. For first and second-year associates, it's pretty much a full-time job.")

> *Overall, what Goldman does exceptionally well is create a team culture. And what that really means is people respect young bankers' opinions and look out for the development of junior bankers. Juniors' opinions count and everyone's included on calls. Analysts and associates are encouraged to contribute. They're not locked in a room running numbers. People expect you to have an opinion. It's a place where people have a very low tolerance for egos and obnoxious behavior. There's no yelling and screaming."*
>
> *- Goldman Sachs insider*

Vice Presidents and MDs (a.k.a. "Bankers")

As you become a banker, you begin to shift from modeling and number crunching to relationship building. This gradual transition happens during the senior associate phase as the associate begins interfacing with existing clients. Ultimately, VPs and MDs spend most of their time and energy finding new clients and servicing existing clients. VPs spend more time managing associates and analysts and the pitchbook creation process than

MDs, but their responsibilities begin to resemble those of MDs at the senior VP level. The typical week for a VP or MD, then, looks quite different from that of an analyst or associate.

Monday

The banker gets a courier package delivered at 6 a.m. to her house and carries this with her to the airport. The package contains several copies of an M&A pitch that she intends to make that day. Her team put the finishing touches on the analysis just a few hours before, while she slept at home. Her schedule that day includes three meetings in Houston and one important pitch in the afternoon. As an oil and gas banker, the banker finds she spend two-thirds of her time flying to Texas and Louisiana, where her clients are clustered. In her morning sales calls, the banker visits with a couple CEOs of different companies, gives them an updated general pitchbook and discusses their businesses and whether they have upcoming financing needs. The third meeting of the day is a lunch meeting with a CFO from a company she led a deal for last year.

The banker's cell phone seems glued to her head as she drives from meeting to meeting, but she turns it off for her final meeting – an M&A pitch to a CEO of an oilfield service company. Afterward, the banker grabs dinner with the company's CFO, and finds her way to her hotel around 9 p.m.

Tuesday

The next day the banker heads to a drafting session at the offices of a law firm downtown. She had gotten up early to read through and review the draft of the prospectus, and made comments in the margins. As her firm is only the co-manager on the deal, she merely brings up issues for the group to consider, and does not lead the discussion, leaving that to the lead manager. After the drafting session, the banker catches an early afternoon flight home, leaving an associate at the drafting session to cover for her.

Wednesday

Back in the office, the banker spends all day on the phone. Flooded with calls, the banker has no time to look at any of the models dropped off in her in-box. Finally, around 6 p.m., she calls the associate and analyst team building an IPO model into her office. For an hour, they go through the numbers, with the banker pointing out problems and missing data items. The associate and analyst leave with a full plate of work ahead. The banker heads home at 8 p.m.

Thursday

The banker is back in the office in the morning to review more models and take some phone calls, but she leaves around noon to catch a flight to make it to a "closing dinner" in Texas. It is time to celebrate one of her successfully managed transactions (it was a follow-on) with the working group. As the lead manager, the banker makes sure that she has plenty of gag gifts for the management team and war stories from the offering to share with the group.

Friday

The banker plans on staying in town to make a few sales visits in the morning. Armed again with pitchbooks, the banker spends a few hours wooing potential clients by discussing merger ideas, financing alternatives and any other relevant transaction that could lead to a fee. Heading home, the banker touches base with her favorite associate to discuss a few models that need work, and what she needs for Monday.

Weekend

Over the weekend, the banker has models couriered to her home, where she goes over the numbers and calls in or messengers her comments and changes to the associate back at the office.

Formulas for Success

The formula for succeeding in banking depends on your role, but some generalizations can be made. The expected qualities of hard work, confidence and dedication ring true in every job, but corporate finance takes these expectations to the nth degree.

Analysts

For the analyst, it is all about keeping your head in the computer, working long hours, and double-checking your work before showing it to bankers. Nothing angers a time-constrained VP more than a young naive analyst who puts together sub-par work. The best analysts are usually well-organized, detail-oriented perfectionists with an endless supply of energy and a positive attitude. Quality of work is key to establishing respect early on, and bankers respect number crunchers who make few mistakes and are not afraid to ask smart, to-the-point questions pertaining to a particular assignment. And, while face time is officially rejected at every bank, bankers tend to frown upon analysts gone before dinner time. A new analyst's best move is to ease into a stressful environment by working hard and learning the ropes as quickly as possible.

Generally, analyst programs last two years although a select few analysts are invited to stay a third year. Then, graduating analysts often leave to attend graduate school or to find another job. In rare cases, an analyst may be promoted directly to associate, bypassing grad school entirely. The experience is not all gloom and doom, as analysts receive a fast-track learning experience on Wall Street, top bonuses, and admission to some of the best business schools in the country. Depending on the firm, Wall Street analysts either join a specific industry or product group, or fall into a category called generalists, which means that they work on deals and pitchbooks for a variety of industry groups and hence learn about a variety of companies in a range of industries.

Associates

New MBA, law, or other grad-school graduates begin as associates. The associate excels by demonstrating an aptitude to learn quickly, work hard, and establish himself or herself early on as a dedicated group member. At the associate level, placement into an industry group typically occurs soon after the training program ends, although some firms such as Citibank offer generalist programs for an extended period. Impressions can form quickly, and a new group member who shows willingness to work hard and late for a group will create a positive impression. Associates are more involved than analysts in client meetings, due diligence meetings, drafting sessions and roadshows. So, associates must be able to socialize with clients well.

Over time, associates spend more time on the road, and supervisors keep an eye on their manner and carriage in front of clients. Sharp comments, confidence and poise in front of clients will at this point do more for an associate than all-nighters and face time. Like analysts, associates have also benefited from the departure of talented candidates from investment banks to hedge funds and private equity shops. Thus, the promotion time from associate to vice president has recently been shortened at many firms. Several I-banks have also started to offer internal private equity or principal investing opportunities to associates—opportunities which were previously available only to officers of the firm (vice presidents or higher). Typically, associates move up to vice president level within three to five years.

Vice Presidents

Depending on the firm, VPs often succeed by showing good managerial skills over deals and transactions, as well as over analysts and associates. VPs ultimately are responsible for pitchbooks and transaction details, therefore becoming managers both in and out of the office. Organization, attention to detail, and strong motivational skills lead to big-sized bonuses. Most important however, is a demonstration of leadership. VPs must win business, convince clients to go ahead with certain deals, handle meetings effectively, and cover for MDs at all times. At regional I-banks, the ability to generate business reigns supreme over other characteristics, whereas Wall Street VPs tend to be both transaction processors and revenue generators.

Managing Directors

Success for an MD comes with industry knowledge, an ability to handle clients, and an ability to find new ones. The MD's most important task includes schmoozing in the industry, finding potential deals, and pitching them with confidence and poise. Public speaking skills, industry awareness, demonstrated experience, and an ability to sell create the best managing directors. Importantly, however, MDs must still be able to grasp the numbers side of the business and be able to explain them to clients. The progression from associate to MD is typically an eight- to 10-year track.

Capital Markets

Although very similar in workload to the day-in-the-life of the corporate finance coverage banker, the capital markets professional has a slightly different lifestyle. Generally speaking, as the capital markets position is more markets-based, the day-to-day work is concentrated into a shorter span of time. For example, an analyst or associate in Equity Capital Markets is likely to be in the office at 8 a.m., or before, to prepare for the market's opening. Although arriving earlier and having a more concentrated day than their coverage counterparts, these individuals tend to leave work earlier and work less on the weekends. Ultimately, the amount of work is generally the same, just concentrated into shorter hours.

But the work done by someone in capital markets tends to be spread across a wide variety of clients. Instead of quarterbacking a particular deal like a coverage or M&A banker would, a capital markets banker is only responsible for a single piece of a transaction. Whereas a coverage deal team might prepare a pitch for a client, it will look to the appropriate capital markets professionals to provide only very particular slides, summarizing trends and transactions in the market.

From analyst to MD, the responsibilities of capital markets bankers do vary. Analysts and associates are usually responsible for maintaining market analysis and research. VPs and MDs are client-facing, providing market updates for clients and attending client pitches with coverage bankers. When a transaction is in the works, the deal team often schedules regular calls between capital markets professionals and company management to keep everyone on the same page.

Naturally, capital markets professionals' pay is very similar to their coverage counterparts. However, because it is not as much a revenue-generating piece of the puzzle, capital markets professionals are not usually paid at the highest ranks of the deal rainmakers on Wall Street. They can still expect remuneration comparable to other corporate finance I-bankers and they still have exceptional earnings potential.

Decrease your T/NJ Ratio

(Time to New Job)

Use the Internet's most targeted job search tools for finance professionals.

Vault Finance Job Board

The most comprehensive and convenient job board for finance professionals. Target your search by area of finance, function, and experience level, and find the job openings that you want. No surfing required.

VaultMatch Resume Database

Vault takes match-making to the next level: post your resume and customize your search by area of finance, experience and more. We'll match job listings with your interests and criteria and e-mail them directly to your inbox.

> the most trusted name in career information™

Institutional Sales and Trading (S&T)

CHAPTER 9

The war zone

If you've ever been to an investment banking trading floor, you've witnessed the chaos. It's usually a lot of swearing, yelling and flashing computer screens: a pressure cooker of stress. Sometimes the floor is a quiet rumble of activity, but when the market takes a nosedive, panic ensues and the volume kicks up a notch. If you haven't been to a trading operation, imagine a football-field sized floor with people sitting nearly on top of one another, televisions blaring CNN news, and a decibel level that resembles a sporting event, not a library. It's highly social, tense, and loud. The atmosphere is what makes the trading floor unique. Traders rely on their market instincts to move millions of dollars, and salespeople spend hours on the phones, schmoozing with clients and yelling for bids from their traders. Deciding what, when, and how much to buy or sell is difficult with millions of dollars at stake.

However, salespeople and traders work much more reasonable hours than research analysts or corporate finance bankers. Rarely does a salesperson or trader venture into the office on a Saturday or Sunday; the trading floor is completely devoid of life on weekends. Any corporate finance analyst who has crossed a trading floor on a Saturday will tell you that the only noises to be heard on the floor are the clocks ticking and the whir of the air conditioner.

Blurring the line between Corporate Finance and S&T: Structuring

Although there are vast differences between S&T and Corporate Finance, with the recent emergence of more complex derivatives trading, the line has been blurred. One such area is Structured Credit. Unlike regular trading of equity or debt, structured credit instruments (such as CDOs and CLOs) take months to structure (much like a corporate finance deal), before they can be traded in the markets. These instruments are usually exceptionally profitable.

Visit the Vault Finance Career Channel at **www.vault.com/finance** – with insider firm profiles, message boards, the Vault Finance Job Board and more.

VAULT CAREER LIBRARY   **103**

Although the products they structure are eventually sold and traded, the lifestyle of those in structuring is very similar to corporate finance. These individuals work long hours, building models, visiting with clients, and writing offering memorandums. However, due to the market-based nature of their products, structurers usually sit on the trading floor and work intricately with sales and trading professionals.

Shop Talk

Here's a quick example of how a salesperson and a trader interact on an emerging market bond trade.

SALESPERSON: Receives a call from a buy-side firm (say, a large mutual fund). The buy-side firm wishes to sell $10 million of a particular Mexican Par government-issued bond (denominated in U.S. dollars). The emerging markets bond salesperson, seated next to the emerging markets traders, stands up in his chair and yells to the relevant trader, "Give me a bid on $10 million Mex Par, six and a quarter, nineteens."

TRADER: "I got 'em at 73 and an eighth."

Translation: I am willing to buy them at a price of $73

5 per $100 of face value. As mentioned, the $10 million represents amount of par value the client wanted to sell, meaning the trader will buy the bonds, paying 73.125 percent of $10 million plus accrued interest (to factor in interest earned between interest payments).

SALESPERSON: "Can't you do any better than that?"

Translation: Please buy at a higher price, as I will get a higher commission.

TRADER: "That's the best I can do. The market is falling right now. You want to sell?"

SALESPERSON: "Done. $10 million."

S&T: A symbiotic relationship?

Institutional sales and trading are highly dependent on one another. The propaganda that you read in glossy firm brochures portrays those in sales and trading as a shiny, happy integrated team environment of professionals working for the client's interests. While often that is true, salespeople and traders frequently clash, disagree, and bicker.

Simply put, salespeople provide the clients for traders, and traders provide the products for sales. Traders would have nobody to trade for without sales, but sales would have nothing to sell without traders. Understanding how a trader makes money and how a salesperson makes money should explain how conflicts can arise.

Traders make money by selling high and buying low (this difference is called the spread). They are buying securities for clients, and these clients filter in through sales. A trader faced with a buy order for a buy-side firm could care less about the performance of the securities once they are sold. He or she just cares about making the spread. In a sell trade, this means selling at the highest price possible. In a buy trade, this means buying at the lowest price possible.

The salesperson, however, has a different incentive. The total return on the trade often determines the money a salesperson makes, so he wants the trader to sell at a low price. The salesperson also wants to be able to offer the client a better price than competing firms in order to get the trade and earn a commission. This of course leads to many interesting situations, and at the extreme, salespeople and traders who eye one another suspiciously.

The personalities

Salespeople possess remarkable communication skills, including outgoing personalities and a smoothness not often seen in traders. Traders sometimes call them bullshit artists while salespeople counter by calling traders quant guys with no personality. Traders are tough, quick, and often consider themselves smarter than salespeople. The salespeople probably know better how to have fun, but the traders win the prize for mental sharpness and the ability to handle stress.

Visit the Vault Finance Career Channel at www.vault.com/finance – with
insider firm profiles, message boards, the Vault Finance Job Board and more.

VAULT CAREER LIBRARY   105

Trading – The Basics

Trading can make or break an investment bank. Without traders to execute buy and sell transactions, no public deal would get done, no liquidity would exist for securities, and no commissions or spreads would accrue to the bank. Traders carry a "book" accounting for the daily revenue that they generate for the firm – down to the dollar.

Liquidity

As discussed earlier, liquidity is the ability to find tradeable securities in the market. When a large number of buyers and sellers co-exist in the market, a stock or bond is said to be highly liquid. Let's take a look at the liquidity of various types of securities.

- **Common stock.** For stock, liquidity depends on the stock's float in the market. Float is the number of shares available for trade in the market (not the total number of shares, which may include unregistered stock) times the stock price. Usually over time, as a company grows and issues more stock, its float and liquidity increase.

- **Bonds** are another story, however. Corporate bonds typically have the most liquidity immediately following the placement of the bonds. After a few months, most bonds trade infrequently, ending up in a few big money managers' portfolios for good. If buyers and sellers want to trade corporate debt, the lack of liquidity will mean that buyers will be forced to pay a liquidity premium, or sellers will be forced to accept a liquidity discount.

- **Government issues.** Government bonds are yet another story. Munis, treasuries, agencies, and other government bonds form an active market with better liquidity than that of corporate bonds. In fact, the largest single traded security in the world is the 30-year U.S. Government bond (known as the Long Bond), although the 10-year note is closing in fast.

- **Syndicated Loans.** Syndicated loans are not nearly as liquid an instrument as their bond counterparts. Institutional loan tranches are generally traded among a much smaller subset of institutional investors and thus are traded in large chunks of millions of dollars. Generally, loan investors take a buy-and-hold strategy, much like portfolio managers of corporate bonds.

- **Derivatives.** There are a myriad of derivatives traded in the markets, some illiquid, others very liquid. This liquidity depends on the type of derivative being traded. Whereas some complex derivatives are one-time solutions for companies or investors, credit default swaps (a type of credit derivative) are becoming exceptionally liquid as the market becomes more complex.

Floor brokers vs. traders

Often when people talk about traders, they imagine frenzied men and women on the floor of a major stock exchange waving a ticket, trying to buy stock. The NYSE is the classic example of a stock exchange bustling with activity as stocks and bonds are traded and auctioned back and forth by floor traders. In fact, these traders are really floor brokers, who follow through with the execution of a stock or bond transaction. Floor brokers receive their orders from traders working for investment banks and brokerage firms.

As opposed to floor brokers, traders work at the offices of brokerage firms, handling orders via phone from salespeople and investors. Traders either call in orders to floor brokers on the exchange floor or sell stock they already own in inventory, through a computerized system. Floor brokers represent buyers and sellers and literally gather near a trading post on the exchange floor to place, buy and sell orders on behalf of their clients. On the floor of the NYSE, these mini-auctions are handled by a specialist, whose job is to ensure the efficiency and fairness of the trades taking place. We will cover the mechanics of a trade later. First, let's discuss the basics of how a trader makes money and carries inventory.

How the trader makes money

There are two general types of traders. The first, the trader that connects institutional investors with the market, is commonly referred to as a "flow" trader or a market-maker. The second, the trader that takes speculative positions in the markets on behalf of a firm or himself, is often referred to as a "proprietary" trader (more on this later). Also, many flow traders do take prop positions, but their primary function is to make markets.

Understanding how flow traders make money is simple. As discussed earlier, these traders buy stocks and bonds at a low price, then sell them for a slightly higher price. They connect buyers and sellers in the markets. This difference is called the bid-ask spread, or, simply, the spread. For example, a bond may be quoted at 99 1/2 bid, 99 5/8 ask. Money managers who wish to buy this bond would have to pay the ask price to the trader, or 99 5/8. It is likely that the trader purchased the bond earlier at 99 1/2, from an investor looking to sell his securities. Therefore, the trader earns the bid-ask spread on a buy/sell transaction. The bid-ask spread here is 1/8 of a dollar, or $0.125, per $100 of bonds. If the trader bought and sold 10,000 bonds (which each have $1,000 face value for a total value of $100 million), the spread earned would amount to $125,000 for the trader. Not bad for a couple of trades.

Spreads vary depending on the security sold. Generally speaking, the more liquidity a stock or bond has, the narrower the spread. Government bonds, the most liquid of all securities, typically trade at spreads of a mere 1/128th of a dollar. That is, a $1,000 trade nets only 78 cents for the trader. However, government bonds (called "govies" for short) trade in huge volumes. So, a $100 million govie trade nets $78,125 to the investment bank—not a bad trade.

Inventory

While the concept of how a flow trader makes money (the bid-ask spread) is eminently simple, actually executing this strategy is a different story. Traders are subject to market movements—bond and stock prices fluctuate constantly. Because the trader's ultimate responsibility is simply to buy low and sell high, this means anticipating and reacting appropriately to dynamic market conditions that often catch even the most experienced people off guard. A trader who has bought securities but has not sold them is said to be carrying inventory.

Suppose, for instance, that a trader purchased stock at $52 7/8, the market bid price, from a money manager selling his stock. The ask was $53 when the trade was executed. Now the trader looks to unload the stock. The trader has committed the firm's money to purchase stock, and therefore has what is called price movement risk. What happens if the stock price falls before she can unload at the current ask price of $53? Obviously, the trader and the firm lose money. Because of this risk, traders attempt to ensure that the bid-ask spread has enough cushion so that when a stock falls, they do not lose money.

The problem with carrying inventory is that security prices can move dramatically. A company announcing bad news may cause such a rush of sell orders that the price may drop significantly. Remember, every trade has two sides, a buyer and a seller. If the price of a stock or bond is falling, the only buyers in the market may be the traders making a market in that security (as opposed to individual investors). These market makers have to judge by instinct and market savvy where to offer to buy the stock back from investors. If they buy at too high a price (a price higher than the trader can sell the stock back for), they can lose big. Banks will lose even more if a stock falls while a trader holds that stock in inventory.

So what happens in a widespread free-falling market? Well, you can just imagine the pandemonium on the trading floor as investors rush to sell their securities however possible. Traders and investors carrying inventory all lose money. At that point, no one knows where the market will bottom out.

On the flip side, in a booming market, carrying inventory consistently leads to making money. In fact, it is almost impossible not to. Any stock or bond held on the books overnight appreciates in value the next day in a strong bull market. This can foster an environment in which poor decisions become overlooked because of the steady upward climb of the markets. Traders buy and sell securities as investors demand. Usually, a trader owns a stock or bond, ready to sell when asked. When a trader owns the security, he is said to be long the security (what we previously called carrying inventory). This is easy enough to understand.

Being long or short

Consider the following, though. Suppose an investor wished to buy a security and called a trader who at the time did not have the security in inventory. In this case, the trader can do one of two things – 1) not execute the trade or 2) sell the security, despite the fact that he or she does not own it.

How does the second scenario work? The trader goes short the security by selling it to the investor without owning it. Where does he get the security? By borrowing the security from someone else.

Let's look at an example. Suppose a client wished to buy 10,000 shares of Microsoft (MSFT) stock, but the trader did not have any MSFT stock to sell. The trader likely would sell shares to the client by borrowing them from elsewhere and doing what is called **short-selling**, or shorting. In such a short transaction, the trader must eventually buy 10,000 shares back of MSFT to replace the shares he borrowed. The trader will then look for sellers of MSFT in the broker-dealer market, and will often indicate to salespeople of his need to buy MSFT shares. (Salespeople may even seek

Visit the Vault Finance Career Channel at **www.vault.com/finance** – with insider firm profiles, message boards, the Vault Finance Job Board and more.

VAULT CAREER LIBRARY   **109**

out their clients who own MSFT, checking to see if they would be willing to sell the stock.)

The problems with shorting or short-selling stock are the opposite of those that one faces by owning the stock. In a long position, traders worry about big price drops – as the value of your inventory declines, you lose money. In a short position, a trader worries that the stock increases in price. He has locked in his selling price upfront, but has not locked in his purchase price. If the price of the stock moves up, then the purchase price moves up as well.

Tracking the trades

Traders keep track of the exact details of every trade they make. Trading assistants often perform this function, detailing the transaction (buy or sell), the amount (number of shares or bonds), the price, the buyer/seller, and the time of the trade. At the end of the day, the compilation of the dollars made/lost for that day is called a profit and loss statement, or **P&L**. The P&L statement is all-important to a trader: daily, weekly, monthly, quarterly – traders know the status of their P&L's for these periods at any given time.

Types of trades

Unbeknownst to most people, traders actually work in two different markets, that is, they buy and sell securities for two different types of customers.

- One is the **inside market**, which is a monopoly market made up only of broker-dealers. Traders actually utilize a special broker screen that posts the prices broker-dealers are willing to buy and sell to each other. This works as an important source of liquidity when a trader needs to buy or sell securities.

- The other is **outside market**, composed of outside customers an investment bank transacts with. These include a diverse range of money managers and investors, or the firm's outside clients. Traders earn the bulk of their profits in the outside market.

Not only do traders at investment banks work in two different markets, but they can make two different types of trades. As mentioned earlier, these include:

- **Client trades.** These are simply trades done on the behest of outside customers. Most traders' jobs are to make a market in a security for the firm's clients. They buy and sell as market forces dictate and pocket the bid-ask spread along the way. The vast majority of traders trade for clients.

- **Proprietary trades.** Sometimes traders are given leeway in terms of what securities they may buy and sell for the firm. Using firm capital, proprietary traders actually trade not to fulfill client demand for stocks and bonds, but to make bets on the market. Thus, prop trading operations make money not normally off the spread, but by taking either a long or short position in a security. Some prop traders trade such obscure things as the yield curve, making bets as the direction that the yield curve will move. Others are arbitragers, who follow the markets and lock in arbitrage profit when market inefficiencies develop. (In a simple example, a market inefficiency would occur if a security, say U.S. government bonds, is trading for different prices in different locales, say in the U.S. vs. the U.K. Actual market inefficiencies these days often involve derivatives and currency exchange rates.). Unlike flow traders, proprietary traders tend to execute fewer transactions, often acting more like a long-term investor than a trader at all. Hedge funds are essentially proprietary trading operations.

A Trader's Cockpit

You may have wondered about the pile of computer gear a trader uses. This impressive mess of technology, which includes half a dozen blinking monitors, represents more technology per square inch than that used by any other professional on Wall Street. Each trader utilizes different information sources, and so has different computer screens spouting out data and news. Typically, though, a trader has the following:

- **Bloomberg machine:** Bloombergs were invented originally only as bond calculators. (The company that makes them was founded by a former Salomon Brothers trader, Michael Bloomberg, now a billionaire who owns a media empire and is the Mayor of NYC.) Today, however, they perform so many intricate and complex functions that they've become ubiquitous on any equity or debt trading floor. In a few quick keystrokes, a trader can access a bond's price, yield, rating, duration, convexity, and literally thousands of other tidbits. Market news, instant messaging, stock information and even e-mail reside real-time on the Bloomberg.

Visit the Vault Finance Career Channel at **www.vault.com/finance** – with insider firm profiles, message boards, the Vault Finance Job Board and more.

VAULT CAREER LIBRARY

111

- **Phone monitor:** Traders' phone systems are almost as complex as the Bloombergs. The phones consist of a touch-screen monitor with a cluster of phone lines. There are multiple screens that a trader can flip to, with direct dialing and secured lines designed to ensure a foolproof means of communicating with investors, floor brokers, salespeople and the like. For example, one Morgan Stanley associate tells of a direct phone line to billionaire George Soros.

- **Small broker screens:** These include monitors posting market prices from other broker-dealers, or investment banks. Traders deal with each other to facilitate client needs and provide a forum for the flow of securities.

- **Large computer monitor:** Typically divided into numerous sections, the general monitor is tailored to a trader's needs. Popular pages include CNN, e-mail, bond market data, sports pages, and internal company research.

Executing a Trade

If you are a retail investor, and call your broker to place an order, how is the trade actually executed? Now that we know the basics of the trading business, we will cover the mechanics of how stocks or bonds are actually traded. We will begin with what is called **small lots trading**, or the trading of relatively small amounts of a security.

Small lots trading

Surprising to many people, the process of completing a small lot transaction differs depending on where the security is traded and what type of security it is.

- For an NYSE-traded stock, the transaction begins with an investor placing the order and ends with the actual transaction being executed on the floor of the New York Stock Exchange. Here, the trade is a physical, as opposed to an electronic one.

- For NASDAQ-traded stocks, the transaction typically originates with an investor placing an order with a broker and ends with that broker selling stock from his current inventory of securities (stocks the broker actually owns). An excellent analogy of this type of market, called an Over-the-Counter (OTC) Market, is that a trader acts like a pawn shop, selling an inventory of securities when a buyer desires, just like the pawn shop owner sells a watch to a store visitor. And, when an investor wishes to sell securities, he or she contacts a trader who willingly purchases them at a price dictated by the trader, just like the pawn shop owner gives prices at which he will buy watches. (As in a pawn shop, the trader makes money through the difference between the buying and selling price, the bid-ask spread.) In the OTC scenario, the actual storage of the securities is electronic, residing inside the trader's computer.

• For bonds, transactions rarely occur in small lots. By convention, most bonds have a face value of $1,000, and orders for one or even 10 bonds are not common. However, the execution of the trade is similar to NASDAQ stocks. Traders carry inventory on their computer and buy and sell on the spot without the need for an NYSE-style trading pit.

The following pages illustrate the execution of a trade on both the NASDAQ and the NYSE stock exchanges. A bond transaction works similarly to a NASDAQ trade.

Here's a look at the actions that take place during a trade of a NASDAQ-listed stock.

NASDAQ

ORDER: You call in an order of 1,000 shares of Microsoft stock to your retail broker. For small orders, you agree on a trade placed at the market. That is, you say you are willing to pay the ask price as it is currently trading in the market.

EXECUTION: First, the retail broker calls the appropriate trader to handle the transaction. The NASDAQ trader, called a market maker, carries an inventory of certain stocks available for purchase.

TRANSACTION: The market maker checks his inventory of stock. If he carries the security, he simply makes the trade, selling the 1,000 shares of Microsoft from his account (the market maker's account) to you. If he does not already own the stock, then he will buy 1,000 shares directly from another market maker and then sell them immediately to you at a slightly higher price than he paid for them.

Here's a look at a trade of a stock listed on the New York Stock Exchange.

NYSE

ORDER: You decide to buy 1,000 shares of GE. You contact your broker and give an order to buy 1,000 shares. The broker tells you the last trade price (65 1/2) and the current quote (65 3/8 bid, 65 5/8 ask) and takes your order to buy 1,000 shares at the market. The broker also notes the volume of stock available for buy and sell, currently 500 X 500 (i.e., 500 shares of GE in demand at the bid and 500 shares of GE available for sale at the ask).

TRANSMITTAL TO THE FLOOR: The order is transmitted from the broker at the I-bank through the NYSE's computer network directly to what are called NYSE specialists (see sidebar) handling the stock.

THE TRADE: The specialist's book displays a new order to buy 1,000 shares of XYZ at the market. At this point, the specialist can fill the order himself from his own account at the last trade price of 65 1/2, or alternatively, he can transact the 1,000 shares trade at 65 5/8. In the latter case, 500 shares would come from the public customer (who had 500 shares of stock available at the bid price) and 500 shares would come from the specialist selling from his own account.

THE TRADE FINALIZED: If the floor specialist elects to trade at 65 5/8, he sends the details of the trade to his back office via the Exchange's computer network and also electronically to the brokerage firm. This officially records the transaction.

The New York Stock Exchange

The New York Stock Exchange (NYSE), the largest exchange in the world, is composed of approximately 2,800 listed stocks with a total market capitalization of about $18 trillion as of September 2004. The NYSE is often referred to as the Big Board. We have all seen the videos of frantic floor brokers scrambling to execute trades in a mass of bodies and seeming confusion. To establish order amidst the chaos, trading in a particular stock occurs at a specific location on the floor (the trading post), so that all buy and sell interests can meet in one place to determine a fair price.

The NYSE hires what are called specialists to oversee the auctioning or trading of particular securities. Specialists match buyers and sellers, but sometimes there is insufficient public interest on one side of a trade (i.e., there is a seller but no buyer, or a buyer and no seller). Since the specialist cannot match the other side of the trade, the Exchange requires the specialist to act as a dealer to buy (or sell) the stock to fill in the gap. According to the NYSE, specialists are directly involved in approximately 10 percent of trades executed on the floor, while they act as the auctioneer the other 90 percent of the time.

Note that while the NYSE is a physical trading floor located at the corner of Wall and Broad streets in lower Manhattan, the NASDAQ is actually a virtual trading arena. Approved NASDAQ dealers make a market in particular stocks by buying and selling shares through a computerized trading system. This is called an over-the-counter system or OTC system, with a network of linked computers acting as the auctioneer.

According to the NYSE's web site, "To buy and sell securities on the Trading Floor, a person must first meet rigorous personal and financial standards and be accepted for membership in the NYSE." Members usually are said to have a seat on the NYSE (though you can be a member without having a seat), but they rarely find time to sit down. Members, like everyone else at the NYSE, are on their feet most of the working day. A seat is simply the traditional term for the right to trade on the NYSE's Trading Floor.

Block trades

Small trades placed through brokers (often called **retail trades**) require a few simple entries into a computer. In these cases, traders record the exchange of a few hundred shares or a few thousand shares, and the trade happens with a few swift keystrokes.

However, when a large institutional investor seeks to buy or sell a large chunk of stock, or a block of stock, the sheer size of the order involves additional facilitation. A buy order for 200,000 shares of IBM stock, for instance, would not easily be accomplished without a block trader. At any given moment, only so much stock is available for sale, and to buy a large quantity would drive the price up in the market (to entice more sellers into the market to sell).

For a NYSE stock, the process of **block trading** is similar to trading any small buy or sell order. The difference is that a small trade arrives electronically to the specialist on the floor of the exchange, while a block trade runs through a floor broker, who then hand-delivers the order to the specialist. The style of a block trade also differs, depending on the client's wishes. Some block trades are done at the market and some block trades involve working the order.

- **At the market.** Say portfolio managers at Fidelity wish to buy 200,000 shares of IBM, and they first contact the block trader at an investment bank. If the Fidelity managers believed that IBM stock was moving up, they would indicate that the purchase of the shares should occur at the market. In this case, the trader would call the floor broker (in reality, he contacts the floor broker's clerk), to tell him or her to buy the next available 200,000 shares of IBM. The clerk delivers the ticket to the floor broker, who then takes it to the specialist dealing in IBM stock. Again, the specialist acts as an auctioneer, matching sellers to the IBM buyer. Once the floor broker accumulates the entire amount of stock, likely from many sellers, his or her clerk is sent back to the phones to call back the trader. The final trading price is a weighted average of all of the purchase prices from the individual sellers.

- **Working the order.** Alternately, if the Fidelity managers believe that IBM was going to bounce around in price, they might ask the trader to work the order so that they get a better price than what is currently in the market. The trader then would call the floor broker and indicate that he or she should work at finding as low a price as possible. In this case, the floor broker might linger at the IBM trading post, watching for sell orders to come in, hoping to accumulate the shares at as low a price as possible.

Trading bonds

Bond trading takes place in OTC fashion, just as stocks do on the NASDAQ. That is, there is no physical trading floor for bonds, merely a collection of linked computers and market makers around the world (literally). As such, there is no central open outcry market floor for bonds, as there is for NYSE stocks. Therefore, for bond orders, the transaction flow is similar to that of an OTC stock. A buyer calls a broker-dealer, indicates the bonds he wishes to buy, and the trader sells the securities with a phone call and a few keystrokes on his computer.

Trading – The Players

Each desk on a trading floor carries its own sub-culture. Some are tougher than others, some work late, and some socialize outside of work on a regular basis. While some new associates in trading maintain ambitions of working on a particular desk because of the product (say, equities or high yield debt), most find themselves in an environment where they most enjoy the people. After all, salespeople and traders sit side-by-side for 10-12 hours a day. Liking the guy in the next chair takes precedence when placing an associate full-time on a desk, especially considering the levels of stress, noise and pressure on a trading floor.

The desk

Different areas on the trading floor at an I-bank typically are divided into groups called "desks." Common desks include OTC equity trading, Big Board (NYSE) equity trading, convertibles (or "converts"), municipal bonds ("munis"), high yield, high grade, interest rates, commodities, foreign exchange (FX for short), proprietary trading, and Treasuries. This list is far from complete—some of the bigger firms have 50 or more distinct trading desks on the floor (depending how they are defined). Investment banks usually separate the equity trading floor from the debt trading floor. In fact, equity traders and debt traders rarely interact. Conversely, sales and trading within one of these departments are combined and integrated as much as possible. For example, treasury salespeople and treasury traders work next to one another on the same desk. Sales will be covered in following sections.

The players

The players in the trading game depend on the firm. There are no hard and fast rules regarding whether or not one needs an MBA in trading. The degree itself, though less applicable directly to the trading position, tends to matter beyond the trader level. Managers (heads of desks) and higher-ups are often selected from the MBA ranks.

Generally, regional I-banks hire clerks and/or trading assistants (non-MBAs) who are sometimes able to advance to a full-fledged trading job within a few years. Other banks, usually the bulge bracket banks, hire analysts and associates just as they do in investment banking. However, much like corporate finance (and happening much more often) it is not uncommon for an associate at a bulge bracket bank to have skipped the b-

Visit the Vault Finance Career Channel at **www.vault.com/finance** – with
insider firm profiles, message boards, the Vault Finance Job Board and more.

VAULT CAREER LIBRARY   **119**

school process altogether. The ultimate job in trading is to become a full-fledged trader or a manager over a trading desk. Here we break out the early positions into those more common at regional I-banks and those more common on Wall Street.

Entry-level positions

Regional Frameworks – Traditional Programs

Clerks. The bottom rung of the ladder in trading in regional firms, clerks generally balance the books, tracking a desk or a particular trader's buy and sell transactions throughout the day. A starting point for an undergrad aiming to move up to an assistant trader role, clerks gain exposure to the trading floor environment, the traders themselves and the markets. However, clerks take messages, make copies, go get coffee, and are hardly respected by traders. And at bigger firms, this position can be a dead-end job: clerks may remain in these roles indefinitely, while new MBAs move into full-time trading positions or graduates of top colleges move into real analyst jobs.

Trading assistants. Typically filled by recent graduates of undergraduate universities, the trading assistant position is more involved in trades than the clerk position. Trading assistants move beyond staring at the computer and balancing the books to become more involved with the actual traders. Backing up accounts, relaying messages and reports to and from the floor of the NYSE, and actually speaking with some accounts occasionally—these responsibilities bring trading assistants much closer to understanding how the whole business works. Depending on the firm, some undergrads immediately move into trading assistant positions with the hope of moving into a full-time trading job.

Note: Clerks and trading assistants at some firms are hired with the possibility of upward advancement. However, unless demonstrating long-term potential, promoting those without analyst experience or advanced degrees to full-time trading jobs is becoming more and more uncommon, even at regional firms.

Wall Street Analyst and Associate Programs

Analysts. Similar to corporate finance analysts, trading analysts at Wall Street firms typically are smart undergraduates with the desire to either become a trader or learn about the trading environment. Quantitative skills are a must for analysts, as much of their time is spent dealing with books of trades and numbers. The ability to crunch numbers in a short time is

© 2007 Vault Inc.

especially important on the debt side. Traders often demand bond price or yield calculations with only a moment's notice, and analysts must be able to produce. After a two- to three-year stint, analysts move on to business school or go to another firm, although promotion to the associate level is much more common in trading than it is in corporate finance. (Salaries generally mirror those paid to corporate finance analysts.)

Associates. Trading associates, typically recent business school graduates or star analysts, begin in either rotational programs or are hired directly to a desk. Rotations can last anywhere from a month to a year, and are designed to both educate new MBAs on various desks and to ensure a good fit prior to placement. New MBAs begin at about $95,000 with a $35,000-$55,000 mid-year bonus at major Wall Street banks (again, much like corporate finance, they are paid this "stub bonus" to get them onto the January-to-January standard pay cycle). Second-year associate compensation also tracks closely to that of the second-year corporate finance associate, with the potential to earn significantly more if the associate becomes a top performer and star trader.. Associates generally move to full-fledged trading positions generally in about two to three years, but can move more quickly if they perform well and there are openings (turnover) on the desk.

As the financial markets have become increasingly complex, many investment banks have even sought to hire PhDs into the ranks of their trading operations as associates, hoping to identify and capitalize on trends in the markets. With an understanding of complex applied math and/or economics, these individuals are capable of executing and understanding the most complex trades in the most complex markets. Many investment banks have entire departments dedicated to quantitative trading and research.

Full-fledged trading positions

Block traders. These are the folks you see sitting on a desk with dozens of phone lines ringing simultaneously and four or more computer monitors blinking, with orders coming in like machine-gun fire. Typically, traders deal in active, mature markets, such as government securities, stocks, currencies and corporate bonds. Sometimes hailing from top MBA schools, and sometimes tough guys named Vinny from the mailroom, traders historically are hired based on work ethic, attitude and street-smarts.

Sales-traders. A hybrid between sales and trading, sales-traders essentially operate in a dual role as both salesperson and block trader. While block traders deal with huge trades and often massive inventories of stocks or bonds, sales-traders act somewhat as a go-between for salespeople and block traders. In this role, they trade somewhat smaller blocks of securities. Different from the pure block trader, the sales-trader actually initiates calls to clients, pitches investment ideas and gives market commentary. The sales-trader keeps abreast of market conditions and research commentaries, but, unlike the salesperson, does not need to know the ins and outs of every company when pitching products to clients. Salespeople must be thoroughly versed in the companies they are pitching to clients, whereas sales-traders typically cover the highlights and the big picture. When specific questions arise, a sales-trader will often refer a client to the research analyst.

Structured product traders. At some of the biggest Wall Street firms, structured product traders deal with derivatives, a.k.a. structured products. (Derivatives are complex securities that derive their value out of, or have their value contingent on, the values of other assets like stocks, bonds, commodity prices, or market index values.) Because of their complexity, derivatives typically require substantial time to price and structure, and thus trading derivatives fosters an entirely different environment than that of block trading, with heavy trading flows and intense on-the-spot pressure. Note, however, that common stock options (calls and puts) and even Treasury options trade much like any other liquid security. The pricing is fairly transparent, the securities standardized and the volume high. Low-volume, complex derivatives such as interest rate swaps, structured repurchase agreements, and credit derivatives require pricing and typically more legwork prior to trading. In contrast to block trading, where trades happen almost instantly, the lifecycle of a trade in structured credit could take up to four weeks or longer.

Note that in trading, job titles can range from Associate to VP to Managing Director. But, the roles as a trader change little. The difference is that MDs typically manage the desks, spending their time dealing with desk issues, risk management issues, personnel issues, etc. Furthermore, traders generally care less about title and more about compensation.

Trader's Compensation: The Bonus Pool

In trading, most firms pay a fixed salary plus a bonus based on the profits the trader brings to the group. Once associates have moved into full-fledged trading roles after two or three years, they begin to be judged by their profit contributions. How much can a trader make? Typically, each desk on the trading floor has a P&L statement for the group. As the group does well, so do the primary contributors. In a down year, everyone suffers. In up years, everyone is happy.

Exactly how the bonuses are determined can be a mystery. Office politics, profits brought into the firm, and tenure all contribute to the final distribution. Often, the MDs on the desk or the top two or three traders on the desk get together and hash out how the bonus pool will be allocated to each person. Then, each trader is told what his or her bonus is. If he or she is unhappy, it is not uncommon for traders (as well as any other employee at an I-bank) to jump ship and leave the firm the second that his or her bonus check clears the bank. Top traders can easily pull in well over $1 million per year. In the past years, it has been rumored that quite a few proprietary traders have cleared in excess of $25 million in bonuses alone. The best traders are usually the best compensated on Wall Street, often earning more than CEOs of Fortune 100 corporations or even top-paid professional athletes.

Trading – The Routine

The compressed day

Instead of working long hours, traders pack more work into an abbreviated day—a sprint instead of the slow marathon that corporate finance bankers endure. Stress, caffeine, and adrenaline keep traders wired to the markets, their screens, and the trades they are developing. While traders typically arrive by 7 a.m., it is not unheard of to make phone calls to overseas markets in the middle of the night or wake up at 4 a.m. to check on the latest market news form Asia. The link among markets worldwide has never been as apparent as in the past several years, and traders, perhaps more so than any other finance professional, must take care to know the implications of a wide variety of global economic and market events.

Visit the Vault Finance Career Channel at **www.vault.com/finance** – with
insider firm profiles, message boards, the Vault Finance Job Board and more.

VAULT CAREER LIBRARY   **123**

Traders consider themselves smarter than the salespeople, who they generally believe don't understand the products they sell, and bankers, who they believe are slaves with no lives whatsoever. Traders take pride in having free weekends without BlackBerry interruption and the option of leaving early on a Friday afternoon. Typically, a trader's day tracks closely to those of the market, and includes an additional two or more hours. Many traders wonder why anyone would become a banker when traders earn as much money, or more, with fewer hours.

Traders' mornings start usually between 6 a.m. and 7 a.m., and the day ends shortly after the market close between 5:30 and 6 p.m.

Traders typically start the day by checking news, reviewing markets that trade overnight (i.e., Asian markets), and examining their inventory. At 7:30 a.m., the morning meeting is held to cover a multitude of issues (see inset).

The Morning Meeting

Every morning of every trading day, each I-banking firm (both on and off Wall Street) holds a morning meeting. What happens at these meetings? Besides coffee all around and a few yawns, morning meetings generally are a way to brief sales, trading, and research on market activity—past and expected.

At smaller regional firms, the entire equity group usually meets: the salesforce, traders, and research analysts. The bigger firms, because of their sheer size, wire speakers to an overhead speaking system, which is broadcast to the entire equity trading floor. Institutional salespeople and brokers outside the home office also call in to listen in on the meeting.

In debt trading, meetings are often broken down by groups. For example, the government desk, the mortgage desk, the emerging markets desk, and the high yield desk will each have their own morning meetings with the relevant traders, salespeople and research analysts present.

Let's take a look at the participants in morning meetings and their roles:

- In equity, the research analysts review updates to their stocks, present new research and generally discuss the scoop on their universe of stocks. Rating changes and initiation of coverage

reports command the most attention to both traders and
salespeople on the equity side. In fixed income, meetings will often
have analysts who cover economic issues discuss interest rates,
Fed activity or market issues, as these often dominate activity in
the debt markets.

- Traders cover their inventory, mainly for the benefit of salespeople
  and brokers in the field. Sometimes a trader eager to move some
  stock or bonds he or she has carried on the books too long will give
  quick selling points and indicate where he or she is willing to sell
  the securities.

- Salespeople, including both brokers and institutional sales,
  primarily listen and ask relevant questions to the research analyst
  or to traders, sometimes chipping in with additional information
  about news or market data.

Morning meetings include rapid-fire discussions on market movements,
positions, and relevant trade ideas. Time is short, however, so a
babbling research analyst will quickly lose the attentions spans of
impatient salespeople.

Conversely, corporate finance professionals rarely attend morning
meetings, choosing instead to show up for work around 9 or 10 a.m.

After the morning meeting, between 8:00 and 8:15 a.m., the traders begin
to gear up for the market opening, while observing the action in extended-
hours trading. At 8:30 a.m., the fun begins in many fixed income markets—
calls begin pouring in and trades start flying. At 9:30 a.m. Eastern Time, the
equity markets open and a flurry of activity immediately ensues.

The day continues with a barrage of market news from the outside, rating
changes from research analysts and phone calls from clients. The first
breather does not come until lunchtime, when traders take five to grab a
sandwich and relax for a few brief minutes. However, the market does not
close at lunch, and if a trade is in progress, the traders go without their
meals or with meals swallowed at their desks amidst the frenzy. Traders
often send an intern to a nearby McDonald's to bring back burgers for the
traders.

The action heats up again after lunchtime and continues as before. At 4
p.m., the equity markets officially close and wrap-up begins. Most traders

Visit the Vault Finance Career Channel at **www.vault.com/finance** – with
insider firm profiles, message boards, the Vault Finance Job Board and more.

VAULT CAREER LIBRARY   **125**

tend to leave around 5 p.m. after closing the books for the day and tying up loose ends. On Fridays, most trading floors are completely empty by 5 p.m. Unlike for bankers, for salespeople and traders, rounds of golf, trips to the bar and other social activities are not usually hampered by Friday evenings and nights spent at work.

A Day in the Life of a Sales-Trader (Lehman Brothers)

Here's a look at a day in the life of a sales-trader, given to us by an associate in the Equities division at Lehman Brothers.

6:30   Get into work. Check voice mail and e-mail. Chat with some people at your desk about the headlines in the Journal.

7:15   Equities morning call. You find out what's up to sell. ("I'm sort of a liaison between the accounts [clients] and the block traders. What I do is help traders execute their trading strategies, give them market color. If they want something I try to find the other side of the trade. Or if I have stuff available, I get info out, without exposing what we have.")

9:30   Markets open. You hit the phones. ("You want to make outgoing calls, you don't really want people to call you. I'm calling my clients, telling them what research is relevant to them, and what merchandise I have, if there's any news on any of their positions.")

10:00   More calls. ("I usually have about 35 different clients. It's always listed equities, but it's a huge range of equities. The client can be a buyer or seller – there's one sales-trader representing a buyer, another representing the seller.")

10:30   On the phone with another Lehman trader, trying to satisfy a client. ("If they have questions in another product, I'll try to help them out.")

11:00   Calling another client. ("It's a trader at the other end, receiving discussions from portfolio manager; their discretion varies from client to client.")

12:00   You hear a call for the sale for a stock that several of your clients are keen on acquiring. ("It's usually a block trader, although sometimes it's another sales-trader. The announcement comes 'over the top,' – over the speaker. It also comes on my computer.")

12:30 Food from the deli comes in. (You can't go to the bathroom sometimes, say you're working 10 orders, you want to see every stock. We don't leave to get our lunch, we order lunch in.")

1:00   Watching your terminal ("There's a lot of action. If there's 200,000 shares trade in your name [a stock that a client has a position in or wants] and it's not you, you want to go back to your client and say who it was.)

2:00   Taking a call from a client. ("You can't miss a beat, you are literally in your seat all day.")

2:05   You tell the client that you have some stock he had indicated interest in previously, but you don't let him know how much you can unload. ("It's a lot of how to get a trade done without disclosing anything that's going to hurt the account. If you have to one stock is up you don't want the whole Street to know, or it'll drive down the price.")

4:30   Head home to rest a bit before going out. ("I leave at 4:30 or sometimes 5:00. It depends.")

7:00   Meet a buy-side trader, one of your clients, at a bar. ("We entertain a lot of buy-side traders – dinner, we go to baseball games, we go to bars. Maybe this happens once or twice a week.")

Success factors in trading

There are many keys to success in trading. On the fixed income side, numbers and quantitative skills are especially important, but truly are a prerequisite to survival more than a factor to success. In equities, traders must not only juggle the numbers, but also understand what drives stock prices. These factors include earnings, management assessments, how news affects stocks, etc.

To be one of the best traders, an instinct about the market is key. Some traders look at technical indicators and numbers until they are blue in the face, but without a gut feel on how the market moves, they will never rank among the best. A trader must make rapid decisions at times with little information to go on, and so must be able to quickly assess investor sentiment, market dynamics and the ins and outs of the securities they are trading.

Institutional Sales - The Basics

Sales is a core area of any investment bank, comprising the vast majority of people and the relationships that account for a substantial portion of any investment banks' revenues. This section illustrates the divisions seen in sales today at most investment banks. Note, however, that many firms, such as Goldman Sachs, identify themselves as institutionally focused I-banks, and do not even have a retail sales distribution network. Goldman, does, however maintain a solid presence in providing brokerage services to the vastly rich in a division called Private Client Services (PCS for short).

Retail Brokers

Some firms call them account executives and some call them financial advisors or financial consultants. Regardless of this official designator, they are still referring to your classic **retail broker**. The broker's job involves managing the account portfolios for individual investors – usually called retail investors. Brokers charge a commission on any stock trade and also give advice to their clients regarding stocks to buy or sell, and when to buy or sell them. To get into the business, retail brokers must have an undergraduate degree and demonstrated sales skills. Passing the Series 7 and Series 63 examinations are also required before selling commences. Being networked to people with money offers a tremendous advantage for a starting broker.

Institutional Sales

Similar to a broker, yet with more market savvy (and often an MBA), the institutional salesperson manages the bank's relationships with institutional money managers such as mutual funds, hedge funds, and pension funds. Institutional sales is often called research sales, as salespeople focus on selling the firm's research to institutions. As in other areas in banking, the typical hire hails from a top business school such as Wharton or HBS and carries a tiptop résumé (that often involves prior sales or corporate finance experience).

Private Client Services (PCS)

A cross between institutional sales and retail brokerage, PCS focuses on providing money management services to extremely wealthy individuals. A client with more than $3 to $5 million in assets usually upgrades from a classic retail broker to a PCS representative. Similar to institutional sales,

PCS generally hires only MBAs with solid selling experience and top credentials for sales positions. Because PCS representatives become high-end relationship managers, as well as money managers and advisors, the job requires greater expertise than the classic retail broker. Also, because PCS clients trade in larger volumes, the fees and commissions are larger and the number of candidates lining up to become PCS reps is longer.

Institutional Sales - The Players

The players in sales

For many, institutional sales offers the best of all worlds: great pay, fewer hours than in corporate finance or research, less stress than in trading, and a nice blend of travel and office work. Like traders, the hours typically follow the market, with a few tacked on at the end of the day after the market closes. Another plus for talented salespeople is that they develop relationships with key money managers. On the downside, many institutional salespeople complain that many buy-siders disregard their calls, that compensation can exhibit volatile mood swings, that they are overeducated for what they do, and that constantly entertaining clients can prove exhausting.

Sales assistants: Sales assistants take on a primarily clerical role on the desk. Series 7 and 63-certified, they are usually hungry undergraduates, eager to make their way onto the desk. Handling the phones, administrative duties, message taking, letter writing—there's nothing glamorous for the assistants. However, if an associate is to leave, an eager sales assistant has as good a shot as anyone else for the position.

Associates: The newly hired MBA is called an associate, or sales associate. Like analogous associates in other investment banking departments, a sales associate spends a year or so in the role learning the ropes and establishing herself. Associates typically spend one to two months rotating through various desks and ensuring a solid fit between the desk and the new associate. Once the rotations end, the associate is placed on a desk and the business of building client relationships begins. As of publication, most sales associates out of business school pull in the standard package on Wall Street: $95,000 base plus bonuses of $35,000-$55,000 in the first six months. Pay escalation in the first year depends on the bonus, which often ranges from 50 percent of salary to 90 percent of salary. Beyond that, compensation packages depend on the firm—most firms pay based on commissions generated for the firm.

Salesperson: The associate moves into a full-fledged salesperson role extremely quickly. Within a few months on a desk, the associate begins to handle "B" accounts and gradually manages them exclusively. A salesperson's ultimate goal is the account at a huge money manager, such as Fidelity, Putnam, or T-Rowe Price that trades in huge volumes on a daily basis. Therefore, a salesperson slowly moves up the account chain, yielding B accounts to younger salespeople and taking on bigger and better "A" accounts. Good salespeople make anywhere from $500,000 to beyond $1 million per year in total compensation. Salespeople usually focus by region. For example, an institutional equity salesperson will cover all of the buy-side firms in one small region of the country like New England, San Francisco or Chicago. Many salespeople cover New York, as the sheer number of money managers in the City makes for a tremendous volume of work. Salespeople work on specific desks on the trading floor next to traders. Because so much of their work overlaps, sales and trading truly go hand-in-hand. Here's a look at how a trade works from the sales perspective:.

The Flow of the Trade: The Sales Perspective

The salesperson has a relationship with a money manager, or an account, as they say. Suppose a research analyst initiates coverage of a new stock with a Buy-1 rating. The salesperson calls the portfolio manager (PM) at the account and gives an overview of the stock and why it is a good buy. The PM will have his own internal research analysts compile a financial model, just as the sell-side research analyst has done, but likely with slightly different expectations and numbers. If the portfolio manager likes the stock, she will contact her trader to work with the trader at the investment bank.

```
┌─────────────────────────────────────────────┐
│   Sell-side research analyst initiates        │
│   Buy-1 coverage of stock XYZ                  │
└─────────────────────────────────────────────┘
                      │
                      ▼
┌─────────────────────────────────────────────┐
│   Institutional salesperson listens to        │
│   analyst present stock at morning meeting.    │
└─────────────────────────────────────────────┘
                      │
                      ▼
```

Institutional salesperson understands key points of stock XYZ and calls the portfolio manager (PM) at the buy-side firm.

↓

Salesperson pitches stock to PM.

↓

PM talks to her internal analyst and discusses potential purchase.

↓

Analyst performs analysis on company XYZ and gets back to PM with a recommendation to buy.

↓

PM calls institutional salesperson, and indicates her desire to buy the stock, also indicating how many shares.

↓

PM contacts her own internal trader, who calls the investment bank's trader to give the official order.

↓

The sell-side trader works the order as described in previous chapters.

Involvement in an IPO

Corporate finance investment bankers would argue that the salesforce does the least work on an IPO and makes the most money. Salespeople, however, truly help place the offering with various money managers. To give you a breakdown, IPOs typically cost the company going public 7 percent of the gross proceeds raised in the offering. That 7 percent is divided among sales, syndicate and investment banking (i.e., corporate finance) in approximately the following manner:

- 60 percent to Sales
- 20 percent to Corporate Finance
- 20 percent to Syndicate

Visit the Vault Finance Career Channel at **www.vault.com/finance** – with
insider firm profiles, message boards, the Vault Finance Job Board and more.

VAULT CAREER LIBRARY   131

(If there are any deal expenses, those get charged to the syndicate account and the profits left over from syndicate get split between the syndicate group and the corporate finance group.)

As we can see from this breakdown, the sales department stands the most to gain from an IPO. Its involvement does not begin, however, until a week or two prior to the roadshow. At that point, salespeople begin brushing up on the offering company, making calls to their accounts, and pitching the deal. Ideally, they are setting up meetings (called one-on-ones when the meetings are private) between the portfolio manager and the management team of the company issuing the offering. During the roadshow itself, salespeople from the lead underwriter often fly out to attend the meeting between the company and the buy-side PM. While their role is limited during the actual meeting, salespeople essentially hold the PMs' hands, convincing them to buy into the offering.

The sales routine

The institutional salesperson's day begins early. Most arrive at 7 a.m. having already read the morning papers. Each day a package of research is delivered to the salesperson's chair, so reading and skimming these reports begins immediately. The morning meeting at 7:30 involves research commentaries and new developments from research analysts. The trading meeting usually begins 20 minutes later, with updates on trading positions and possible bargains for salespeople to pitch.

At 8 a.m., the salesperson picks up the phone. Calls initially go to the most important of clients, or the bigger clients wishing to get a market overview before trading begins. As the market approaches the opening bell, the salesperson finishes the morning calls and gets ready for the market opening. Some morning calls involve buy or sell ideas, while others involve market updates and stock expectations. At 9:30, the markets open for business, and salespeople continue to call clients, scrutinize the market, and especially look for trading ideas throughout the day.

Lunchtime is less critical to the salesperson than the trader, although most tend to eat at their desk on the floor. The afternoon often involves more contacting buy-siders regarding trade ideas, as new updates arrive by the minute from research.

Day in the Life of a Sales Associate (Bear Stearns)

Here's a look at a day in the life of a sales associate in the Fixed Income division at Bear Stearns in New York.

6:45   Get to work. ("I try to get in around 6:45. Sometimes it's 7:00.)

6:50   After checking e-mail and voice mail, start looking over The Wall Street Journal. ("I get most of my sales ideas from The Wall Street Journal. I'd say 70 to 75 percent of my ideas. I also read the Economist, Business Week, just for an overview, some Barron's and the Financial Times. Maybe three issues out of the five for the week for FT.")

7:15   Start checking Bloombergs, getting warmed up, going over your ideas and figuring out where things stand.

7:45   Meet with your group in a conference room for a brief meeting to go over stuff. ("We go over the traders' axe [what the traders will focus on that day], go over research, what the market quotes are on a particular issue.")

8:15   Get back to desk, and get ready to start pitching ideas.

9:15   Have a short meeting with your smaller group.

10:00   One of your clients calls to ask about bonds from a particular company. You tell her you'll get right back to her. Walk over to talk to an analyst who covers that company. ("I'm in contact a lot with my analyst. I listen to my analyst.")

10:15   Back on the horn with your client.

12:30   Run out to lunch with another salesperson from your group. ("We often buy each other lunch. Sometimes to celebrate a big deal we'll order in lunch. We usually go to Little Italy Pizza Place, or Cosi's Sandwiches. It's always the same people, and it's always the same six places.")

1:00   Back at your desk, check voice mail. ("If I leave for 30 minutes or so, when I get back, I'll have five messages.)

2:00   One of your clients wants to make a move. ("I trade something every day. Maybe anywhere from one to 10 trades. It's on a rolling basis. You plant seeds, and maybe someday one of them grows into a trade.")

3:15   Another client calls and wants to place an order.

5:30   Still on the phone. ("Although the markets close, that's when you can really take the time to talk about where things are and why you think someone should do something.")

7:30   Head for home, you're meeting a client for a late dinner. ("Often on Thursdays we go out as a group.")

The regular session of the major equity markets closes abruptly after 4:00 p.m. By 4:01, many salespeople have fled the building, although many put in a couple more hours of work. Salespeople often entertain buy-side clients in the evening with ball games, fancy dinners, etc.

Success factors in institutional sales

Early on, new associates must demonstrate an ability to get along with the clients they are asked to handle. Usually, the first-year sales associate plays second string to the senior salesperson's account. Any perception that the young salesperson does not get along with the PM or buy-side analyst means he or she may be immediately yanked from the account. Personality, the ability to learn quickly, and the ability to fit into the sales group will ensure movement up the ladder. The timing of the career path in sales, more so than in corporate finance, depends on the firm. Some firms trust sales associates quickly with accounts, relying on a sink-or-swim culture. Others, especially the biggest I-banks, wait until they are absolutely sure that the sales associate knows the account and what is going on, before handing over accounts.

Once the level of full-on salesperson is reached (usually after one year to one-and-a-half years on the desk), the goal shifts to growing accounts and successfully managing relationships. Developing and managing the relationships at the various buy-side firms is especially critical. Buysiders can be thought of as time-constrained, wary investors who follow a regimented investing philosophy. Importantly, salespeople must know how and when to contact the investor. For example, a portfolio manager with a goal of finding growth technology stocks will cringe every time a salesperson calls with anything outside of that focused area. Therefore, the salesperson carefully funnels only the most relevant information to the client.

Promotions depend on a combination of individual performance and desk performance. The ability to handle relationships, to bring in new clients, and to generate commission sales for the firm are paramount. Those that have managed to join the ranks of institutional sales without an MBA may be at a disadvantage when it comes to promotions into management roles.

Private Client Services (PCS)

The private client services (PCS) job can be exhilarating, exhausting and frustrating – all at once. As a PCS representative, your job is to bring in individual accounts with at least $2 to $3 million in assets. This involves incessantly pounding the pavement and reading the tape (market news) to find clients, followed by advising them on how to manage their wealth. PCS is a highly entrepreneurial environment. Building the book is all that matters, and managers don't care how a PCS representative spends his or her time, whether this be on the road, in the office, or at parties – the goal is to bring in the cash. Culture-wise, therefore, one typically finds a spirited entrepreneurial group of people, working their own hours and talking on the phone for the better part of the day. It is not uncommon for PCS pros to leave the office early on Fridays with a golf bag slung over one shoulder for a game with existing clients or with a few bigshots with money to invest (read: potential clients).

The growth in PCS

Just a few years ago, PCS was considered a small, unimportant aspect of investment banking. PCS guys were essentially retail brokers, always bothering other departments for leads and not as sophisticated as their counterparts in corporate finance or institutional sales and trading. Times have changed, however. Today, spurred by the tremendous stock market wealth that has been created over the past few years, PCS is a rapidly growing part of virtually every investment bank. While in the past, many banks essentially had no PCS division, or simply hired a few star retail brokers to be PCS representatives, Wall Street is recruiting heavily on top-tier MBA campuses today, scouring to find good talent for PCS.

Getting in the door

It takes an MBA these days, or a stellar record as a retail broker to become a private client sales representative. Even firms such as Merrill Lynch, which historically promoted retail brokers to the PCS role, are moving more and more toward hiring only those with business degrees from top schools and proven selling credentials, rather than proven brokers. PCS is also evolving into an entirely different business from traditional retail brokerage.

Whereas retail brokers make money on commissions generated through trades, PCS reps are increasingly charging clients just as money managers do – as a percentage of assets under management. A typical fee might be 1 percent per year of total assets under management. This fee obviously increases as the value of the assets increases, thereby motivating the PCS worker to generate solid returns on the portfolio. This move to fee-based management is designed to take away the incentive of a salesperson to churn or trade an account just for the sake of the commissions. One should note, however, that the trend to charge a fee instead of commissions is just that – a trend. Many Wall Street PCS reps still work on a commission basis.

The associate position

Once in the door, as a PCS associate, extensive training begins. The PCS associate must be well versed in all areas of the market and able to understand a wide variety of investing strategies. While a corporate bond salesperson has to know only corporate bonds, a PCS rep must be able to discuss the big picture of the market, equities, bonds, and even a slew of derivative products. At any given moment, a very wealthy client might want instant information on any number of products or markets. Thus, training is said to be intensive in PCS, with many weeks of classroom learning.

Once training is complete, a new PCS associate often works to find his way onto a team, which pairs PCS beginners with one or two experienced PCS reps. The process of matching a new associate onto a team is driven largely by personality and fit. Once paired with an older rep or two, the associate works to understand the process of finding new clients and managing a portfolio of assets.

Generally speaking, PCS hires are given two years to build a book, or establish a reasonable level of business for the firm. While salaries for PCS associates out of business school matches those of other Wall Street hires ($95,000 plus a $35,000-$55,000 bonus in the first six months), they quickly are shifted to a straight commission basis. The first years of PCS are the most important when building a long-lasting career in the industry.

How to Build a Book

PCS associates must establish themselves in the first two years through any means possible. Once established, the game changes to managing relationships and using these relationships to gain new clients. Typically, once the PCS associate has learned how to pitch to clients and how to give money-management advice, he or she begins to look for leads. As PCS is a sales job, leads and clients are developed just like at any other sales job. Phone calls, networking and visiting potential clients are key. Ultimately, converting these leads into long-term clients is the name of the game. To find leads, associates might do any of the following:

• Read the tape (follow market news). Many news articles in the markets discuss companies merging, companies going public, companies selling out, management selling stock in their companies, etc. In these cases, there often are CEOs and others on the management team who will find themselves with gobs of cash that must be invested. These are excellent sources of leads.

• Follow up with leads from other areas within the investment bank. A substantial number of corporate finance bankers represent management teams selling stock in public offerings, or selling stock in mergers. The real bonus is that the bankers already know the CEO or CFO with newfound wealth, and can provide an excellent introduction.

• Network. The power of being a friend of a friend cannot be underestimated. That is why PCS reps spend time at parties, functions, on the golf course, and anywhere else they can find leads. Often an "in" such as an introduction provided by a personal friend is the best lead of all.

Pay beyond the associate level

After a successful client list has been established, the sky is the limit in terms of pay. The best of the best PCS pros can easily earn well over a $1 million a year, developing long-lasting deep relationships with a number of wealthy clients. The bottom-of-the-barrel PCS reps, however, may take home a mere $150,000 or so. The average number is somewhere around $500,000 for a PCS pro working for a Wall Street firm. Insiders say it takes an average of five or six years to reach that level, however. Still, there are

Visit the Vault Finance Career Channel at **www.vault.com/finance** – with insider firm profiles, message boards, the Vault Finance Job Board and more.

VAULT CAREER LIBRARY   **137**

exceptions. One insider at Goldman Sachs reports that a PCS representative with that firm reached $3.4 million in compensation only five years out of business school.

Managing the portfolio

You may wonder how a PCS representative with a substantial client base and millions of dollars under account manages all these assets. It actually depends on the firm. Some firms break the PCS job into relationship managers and portfolio managers. For example, at JPMorgan Chase, some PCS reps solely manage the portfolios of the various accounts, and are even paid a straight salary and bonus, depending on returns, while other reps work on client relations. Other firms, with newly built or bought asset management divisions, are attempting to pair PCS and AM (asset management) in order to utilize the existing money management expertise. Goldman Sachs, for example, has sought to do this, but cultural differences between the divisions and the ingrained modus operandi may be a hindrance. Regardless of how the portfolio is managed, the movement toward teams will be a key to melding asset management and relationship management expertise on Wall Street.

Key success factors in PCS

One should keep in mind that PCS divisions essentially want to hire good salespeople, not good number crunchers. They don't need or want quant jocks in PCS; they want salespeople and schmoozers to find and land new clients. The key to succeeding in PCS is generating more assets to manage.

Good PCS reps will manage their client relationships extremely well, as these clients become the bread and butter for them over time. Understanding the goals of clients and executing them are extremely important. For example, one finds in PCS that some investors are not out to beat the S&P at all, and would rather earn steady returns without risking their principal. Remember, a wealthy and retired ex-CEO may not care that his $100 million jackpot beats the market. After all, he's got much more than he could spend in a lifetime. Lower risk and decent returns work just fine in some cases, and PCS representatives must be attuned to these individual differences.

Research

If you have a brokerage account, you have likely been given access to research on stocks that you asked about. This research was probably written by an investment banks' research department or by an independent research arm of the brokerage firm..

To the outsider, it seems that research analysts spend their time in a quiet room poring over numbers, calling companies, and writing research reports. The truth is an entirely different story, involving quite a bit of selling on the phone and on the road. In fact, research analysts produce research ideas, hand them to associates and assistants, and then man the phone talking to buy-side stock/bond pickers, company managers, and internal salespeople. (In the world of research, the "analyst" is the highest ranking position.) They become the managers of research reports and the experts on their industries to the outside world. Thus, while the lifestyle of the research analyst would initially appear to resemble that of a statistician, it often comes closer to that of a diplomat or salesperson.

The Players and The Product

The players

Research assistants
The bottom-level number crunchers in research, research assistants generally begin with no industry or market expertise. They come from solid undergraduate schools and performed well in school, but initially perform mundane research tasks, such as digging up information and editing/formatting reports. Research assistants also take over the spreadsheet modeling functions, updating company models for quarterly numbers or revised earnings estimates. Travel is limited for the budding research assistant, as it usually does not make sense financially to send more than the research analyst to meetings with company officials or money managers.

Research associates
Burdened with numbers and deadlines, the research associate often feels like a cross between a statistician and a corporate finance analyst. Long hours, weekends in the office and number-crunching sum up the routine of

the associate. However, compared to analyst and associate analogues in corporate finance, the research associate works fewer hours, often makes it home at a reasonable time, and works less on the weekend. Unfortunately, the associate is required to be present and accounted for at 7:30 a.m., when most morning meetings on the trading floor take place.

Mirroring the corporate finance analyst and associate positions, research associates can be bright, motivated kids directly out of top undergraduate universities. At firms dedicated to hiring MBAs in research, the research associate role is the entry-level position once the MBA has been earned.

A talented research associate can earn much in the way of responsibility. For example, the research associate may field phone calls from smaller "B" accounts (i.e., smaller money managers) and companies less important to the analyst. (The analyst handles the relationships with the biggest buy-siders, best clients and top salespeople.) When it comes to writing reports, some analysts give free reign to associates in writing. Also, research associates focus on one industry and typically work for only one full-fledged research analyst. This structure helps research associates delve deeper into the aspects of one industry group and enable them to work closely with a senior-level research analyst.

To start, research assistants/associates out of undergraduate typically get paid similarly to the corporate finance analyst right out of college. After one or two years, the compensation varies dramatically, depending on performance and the success of the analysts in the industry group as well as the associate's contribution. For the MBA research associate, the compensation is similar to I-banking associates: as of this writing, $95,000 salaries with $35,000 signing bonuses, plus a $35,000-$55,000 year-end stub bonus, are typical. In many cases, top-tier research assistants are plucked from investment banks to join hedge funds and other money managers, where they are paid for the value of their ideas, not just according to the bank's pay schedule.

It All Depends on the Analyst

Insiders stress that the research associate's contribution entirely depends on the particular analyst. Good analysts (from the perspective of the associate) encourage responsibility and hand-off a significant amount of work. Others communicate poorly, maintain rigid control and don't trust their assistants and associates to do much more than the most mundane tasks.

Being stuck with a mediocre analyst can make your job miserable. If you are considering an entry-level position in research, you should carefully evaluate the research analyst you will work with, as this person will have a huge impact on your job experience.

Note that in research, the job titles for analyst and associate have switched. In corporate finance, one begins as an analyst, and is promoted to associate post-MBA. In research, one begins as a research associate, and ultimately is promoted to the research analyst title.

Research analysts

The research analyst, especially in equity, is truly a guru. Analysts follow particular industries, recommend stocks to buy and sell, and convince salespeople and buy-siders why they or their clients should or should not invest in Company XYZ. The road to becoming an analyst is either paved with solid industry experience, or through the research assistant/associate path.

Full-fledged analyst positions are difficult to come by. The skills required to succeed as an analyst include a firm grasp of: 1) the industry and dynamics of stock picking, and 2) the sales skills required to convince investors and insiders alike why a stock is such an excellent buy. An analyst lacking in either area will simply not become the next *II*-rated star (that is, an analyst highly rated by the annual *Institutional Investor* poll).

Research analysts spend considerable time talking on the phone to investors, salespeople and traders, pitching buy and sell ideas or simply discussing industry or company trends. Everyone tries to get the research analyst's ear, to ask for advice or (as we will discuss in-depth later) to pressure him or her to change a rating or initiate coverage of a particular stock. Although illegal, many hedge funds have come under intense scrutiny after allegedly pressuring influential research analysts for insight on their upcoming company research reports before the reports are published for the market (with the intent to trade on this information).

Visit the Vault Finance Career Channel at **www.vault.com/finance** – with insider firm profiles, message boards, the Vault Finance Job Board and more.

VAULT CAREER LIBRARY

141

Analysts also travel regularly, visiting buy-siders or big money managers and companies in their field. Indirectly, they are trying to generate trading business with money managers, research ideas from companies or trying to build a reputation in the industry. All in all, analysts must be able to pitch an idea convincingly and quickly, and defend it thoroughly when the time comes.

In this atmosphere, research analysts must scrutinize every company that they maintain under coverage. Any news or company announcements will spur a deluge of phone calls to the analyst, with questions ranging from the big picture to the tiniest of details. They also must maintain a handle on an extremely important aspect of any company – the numbers. Inaccurate earnings estimates, especially when they are far from the mark, reflect poorly on the analyst. Why didn't an analyst know the company stock was going to come out with such low earnings? Or, why didn't the research analyst know that industry growth was slowing down? The analyst is responsible for staying on top of these things.

Compensation packages for research analysts run the gamut. Some *II*-rated star analysts in hot industries command multimillion dollar annual packages, especially during bull markets. Most banks figure their compensation for analysts with formulas that are usually incomprehensible to even the research analysts. The factors that go into analyst compensation typically includes a mix of the following:

- The performance of stocks under coverage (meaning that if their stocks perform like the analyst predicts, they get paid well)

- Trading activity within the firm of stocks under coverage

- Corporate finance business revenues of companies in their industry

- Performance evaluations of the research analyst by superiors

- *Institutional Investor* rankings (Once a research analyst finds himself listed as an *II*-ranked analyst, the first stop is into his boss's office to renegotiate his annual package.)

Note: As they progress in their career, research analysts receive titles similar to investment bankers, namely VP, SVP and ultimately MD. However, the tasks of a research analyst tend to remain somewhat consistent once the analyst level is reached, with perhaps more selling of research and traveling involved at the most senior levels, and more oversight of a group of more junior analysts.

The Institutional Investor (II)
Ratings Scorecard

Institutional Investor is a monthly magazine publication that, among other things, rates research analysts. The importance of the II ratings to investment banks and even many institutional investors cannot be overstated. Most industry watchers believe and follow the ratings as if they were gospel.

How do the ratings work? Essentially, II utilizes a formula to determine the best research analysts on Wall Street, surveys industry professionals, and publishes their rankings annually. Note the bias, however, toward research analysts at bulge bracket firms in these ratings. II's formula essentially involves surveys of "directors of research, chief investment officers, portfolio managers, and buy-side analysts at the major money management institutions around the world." Major money managers deal primarily with large investment banks for their trading needs and a portion of their research needs.

In 2006 Lehman Brothers reclaimed its top spot in the II All-America sales rankings. Bear Stearns finished close behind at #2. Citigroup and Merrill Lynch both reclaimed their spots at #3 and #4. UBS rounded out the top 5, moving up a spot from its 6th place finish in 2005. In addition to an overall rankings, II also publishes a variety of industry and categorical rankings.

The product

Industry research reports

To establish oneself as a knowledgeable analyst, many researchers begin by writing and issuing an industry piece. For example, an industry research report on the oil and gas sector might discuss issues such as commodity prices, the general outlook for the sector and valuations of companies in the industry.

The time required to generate an industry piece depends on the length of the report, the complexity of the industry, and how important it is to show expertise to investors and management teams in the industry. For completely new industries for new analysts, a full six months or more is given to enable the analyst to fully understand the industry and develop a thorough report. Once it is printed, salespeople will use an industry research report to get up to speed and learn about a particular segment.

Visit the Vault Finance Career Channel at **www.vault.com/finance** – with insider firm profiles, message boards, the Vault Finance Job Board and more.

VAULT CAREER LIBRARY **143**

Touted as industry expertise, industry research reports take substantial time to produce and earn the firm nothing except awareness that the investment bank follows an industry and has expertise in that industry. However, the brand equity built by an industry piece can be substantial and make cold-calling by bankers a much easier process. With brand equity, the company's foot is already in the door with most clients.

Company-specific research reports

Once an analyst's industry piece has been written and digested by the investment community, the analyst focuses on publishing research reports on specific companies. To create a well-rounded research universe, research analysts will typically write on the top industry players, as well as several smaller players in the industry. One of the most critical roles of an equity research analyst is to make future earnings estimates for the companies he or she covers. (The average earnings estimate of all analysts covering a company is called the "consensus" estimate.) Company-specific reports fall into three categories: initiation of coverage, updates and rating changes.

Initiation of coverage: This is exactly what it sounds like. These reports indicate that an analyst has not previously written research or covered the particular company. Usually an initiation of coverage report includes substantial information about the business, a detailed forecast model and risk factors inherent in the business.

Update: When a stock moves, news/earnings are released, or the analyst meets with management, an update report is put out. Often one-pagers, updates provide quick information important to current movements in the stock or will raise or lower earnings estimates.

Change of rating: Whenever an I-bank alters its rating on a stock (we will discuss these ratings later), a report is issued. These reports vary in length from one to five pages. Reasons for a downgrade include: lower than expected earnings, forecasts for diminished industry or firm growth, management departures, problems integrating a merger, or even overpriced stocks. Reasons for an upgrade include: better than expected earnings, new management, stock repurchases, or beneficial industry trends.

Conflict of Interest

A monumental securities investigation came to end in 2002, forever altering the way investment banks do business. In December 2002, 10 of Wall Street's largest investment firms agreed to pay $1.4 billion to settle research and advisory conflicts-of-interest violations. The settlement closed an investigation that was initially opened by New York State Attorney General Eliot Spitzer, which began in early 2002 with an investigation into research practices at banking behemoth Merrill Lynch. Spitzer alleged that research analysts there allowed potential investment banking fees to influence the ratings given to companies covered by the firm. Since the settlement, considerable action has been taken on the behalf of investment banks to separate their corporate finance operations from their sales, trading, and research operations. As the corporate finance investment bankers often have material non-public company information, this could create a potential conflict of interest if it found its way into the hands of those on the public side of the markets (i.e. sales, trading, and research). This bifurcation of public versus private is known as the "Chinese Wall." Many firms cannot even e-mail between these areas of the bank, due to corporate restrictions in an effort to avoid similar situations.

Market commentary

Analysts usually cover a particular (small) universe of stocks, but some analysts, called market strategists, survey and report on market conditions as a whole. Most large banks publish market commentary reports on a daily basis (sometimes even several within a day), augmented with weekly, monthly and quarterly reviews. Included in such reports is information on the performance of stocks in major market indices in the U.S., major markets worldwide, and in various sectors – such as transportation, technology and energy – in the U.S. Some of these commentaries offer forecasts for the markets or for particular sectors. Naturally, economic data is paramount to stock market performance overall and thus pervades market commentaries.

Economic commentary

Similar to a market commentary, economic reports are also published periodically and cover economic indicators and trends. These reports are often stuffed with graphs of macroeconomic factors such as GDP, inflation, interest rates, consumer spending, new home sales, import/export data, etc.

They provide useful information regarding government fiscal and monetary policy, and often link to fixed income reports. Often the same market strategist writes both the economic commentaries and the market commentaries for a firm.

Fixed income commentary

Analysts covering the fixed income markets publish periodic reports on the debt markets. Often tied to the economic commentaries, fixed income market reports comment on the performance of various fixed income instruments including U.S. government securities, mortgages, corporate bonds, commodity prices and other specialized fixed income securities. The three-point scale for rating stocks has become ubiquitous in banking (since the conflicts-of-interest settlement), but the definitions that banks refer to do not accurately measure what the analyst believes. The following scale reflects the general consensus on stock ratings. However, keep in mind that these ratings vary by firm.

Rating	Published Definition	Actual Meaning
Outperform	STRONG BUY. The company's stock is a strong buy, and will outperform the market over the next 18 months.	The stock is a worthy buy. Or, if the investment bank writing the research just completed a transaction for the company, the analyst may simply believe it is a decent company that will perform as well as the market in the next 18 months.
Neutral	MARKET PERFORM. The stock will perform approximately as well as the market over the next 18 months.	Be wary about buying this stock. It is either richly valued or has potential problems which will inhibit the firm's growth over the next 18 months.
Underperfom	SELL. The stock will perform below the market over the next 18 months	Dump this stock as soon as possible. An underperform rating issued by an analyst means the company is not moving in the right direction.

Three Months in Research

The cycle

Many research analysts comment that there's not a typical day, nor even a typical week in research. On the equity side, the workload is highly cyclical. Everything revolves around earnings reports, which come out quarterly during **earnings season**. The importance of the earnings figures to the stock analyst cannot be stressed enough, and once a quarter, when companies report their earnings data, the job often gets a little crazy.

On the fixed income side, the workflow depends entirely on the product. A high yield or high grade corporate bond research analyst may have some ups and downs in the workload based on the earnings season, but earnings reports are not nearly as critical and as much of a fire drill as they are to equity analysts. We will cover a typical day in debt research in an abbreviated form at end of this chapter. First we'll take a look at a three-month period for an equity research analyst.

While we will focus on the analyst himself, keep in mind that the research associate will also perform many of the same tasks, helping the analyst in any way possible.

March

On March 1, four weeks prior to the end of the quarter (March 31), the analyst begins to look at the financial models relating to the companies under coverage. He is worried about his stocks' earnings per share numbers, which will be reported approximately two to four weeks after the quarter's end. If the estimated EPS numbers stray too far from the actual reported EPS when it comes out, the analyst will find himself dealing with many angry investors and salespeople, at the very least.

To finetune his earnings estimates, the analyst begins calling the companies that he covers, testing assumptions, reading between the lines of recent presentations by company management, refining certain predictions, and generally trying to grasp exactly where the company and industry stand. Details make the difference, and the analyst discusses with the company CFO gross margin estimates, revenue predictions, and even tax issues, to arrive at an acceptable EPS figure. Conversations such as these can become excruciatingly detailed.

April

The quarter has ended, and in early April the research analyst enters the quiet period. During this time companies are restricted from discussing their upcoming earnings release, as this may constitute sensitive inside information. The calm before the storm, the quiet period (in this case, early April) finds many analysts calling other contacts in the industry to discuss broader trends and recent developments in the field.

Once companies begin reporting earnings (which starts mid-month), the analyst scrambles to quickly digest the information and issue one-page update reports. The deluge of company earnings releases causes long and hectic days for the analyst, who must deal with a barrage of phone calls and the demand for written reports from salespeople and institutional investors. Within two weeks after the earnings release, the analyst will typically publish another three-page report on his companies, often with new ratings, new analysis and revised earnings estimates for the next few quarters. During these two weeks, before the reports are released, it is not uncommon for analysts to get pressured by hedge funds for indications of their reports. Such practice is illegal, but definitely not uncommon.

May

In early May, the analyst finishes writing update reports and is afforded a little breathing room. While earnings season involves putting out fires left and right, the end of the reporting period means the analyst can relax and get back to working on long-term projects. These might include industry pieces, initiation reports or other long-term projects. Banks with large corporate finance businesses may encourage their research analysts and associates to spend time working with investment bankers, developing leads, advising them on whom to target, and performing a variety of other research tasks.

Writing the report

Where do new research ideas come from? And when and why do analysts change their ratings?

Frankly, many young analysts are told what companies or areas to cover – until one becomes a seasoned analyst, an analyst focuses on ideas based on firm demands. Veteran analysts with more leeway generate ideas either through industry knowledge or new stocks. Typically, investment banks will compel an analyst to follow a particular stock but will not dictate the rating assigned to the stock. The pressure to publish certain ratings, however, is real and cannot be understated, as it can come from all angles.

The writing process is straightforward, and really depends on the type of report needed. For the inch-thick industry report, for example, research analysts utilize research associates and assistants to the utmost. Analysts coordinate the direction, thesis, and basic content of the report, and do much of the writing. For an introductory initiation of coverage report, the work parallels the industry piece. Substantial research, financial analysis and information gathering requires much time and effort. Behind the scenes, management interviews and company visits to understand and probe the business render the biggest volume of data.

For less labor-intensive pieces, such as changes in ratings or updates, either the analyst or the associate whips out the report in short time. Keep in mind that the analyst usually produces the idea and reviews the report prior to press time, but the associate may in reality put together the entire piece (and put the analyst's name on top).

For all of these reports, research associates and assistants typically find data, compile other research, edit the written material, build financial models and construct graphs and charts of relevant information. The analyst utilizes his or her contacts within the industry to interview insiders to get a glimpse of the latest trends and current events.

Travel

You'd better like suitcases and hotel rooms if you're aiming for a research analyst position—the position requires a great deal of travel. Usually, the full-fledged analyst (as opposed to the associate) does most of the work requiring travel, including meeting with money managers (the buy-side clients) and company management, as well as accompanying corporate finance professionals on roadshows. However, associates will fill in for unavailable analysts, attend some due diligence meetings, and attend conferences and trade shows.

These occasional outside meetings aside, research associates spend almost all of their time in the home office. On the plus side, many associates often meet with managers of the companies that come to visit the bank, meaning research associates have the luxury of meeting one-on-one with top management teams and investor relations representatives. This is especially the case in New York, where research analysts with big firms carry a lot of influence.

Commonly Used Ratios in Research

Solvency Ratios

Quick Ratio =	$\dfrac{\text{Cash} + \text{Accts Rec}}{\text{Total Current Liabilities}}$	Shows the dollars of liquid assets (convertible into cash within 30 days) available to cover each dollar of current debt.
Current Ratio =	$\dfrac{\text{Total Current Assets}}{\text{Total Current Liabilities}}$	Measures the margin of safety present to cover any possible reduction of current assets.
Current Liabilities to Net Worth	$= \dfrac{\text{Total Current Liabilities}}{\text{Net Worth}}$	Contrasts the amounts due creditors within a year with the funds permanently invested by owners. The smaller the net worth and the larger the liabilities, the greater the risk.
Current Liabilities to Inventory	$= \dfrac{\text{Total Liabilities}}{\text{Net Worth}}$	Compares the company's total indebtedness to the venture capital invested by the owners. High debt levels can indicate greater risk.
Fixed Assets to Net Worth = Fixed Assets Net Worth		Reflects the portion of net worth that consists of fixed assets. Generally, a smaller ratio is desired.
Interest Coverage = EBITDA / Interest Expense		Uses EBITDA as a proxy for cash flow to understand a company's ability to meet its debt obligations
Leverage = Total Debt / EBITDA		Reflects the amount of debt in relation to the amount of cash flow (again, using EBITDA as a proxy) for a company's cash flow.

* Net Working Capital = Current Assets—Current Liabilities
Source: Dun & Bradstreet

Efficiency Ratios

Collection Period =	$\dfrac{\text{Accounts Receivable x 365}}{\text{Sales}}$	Reflects the average number of days it takes to collect receivables
Inventory Turnover =	$\dfrac{\text{Sales}}{\text{Inventory}}$	Determine the rate at which merchandise is being moved and the effect of the flow of funds into a business.
Assets to Sales =	$\dfrac{\text{Total Assets}}{\text{Sales}}$	This rate ties in sales and the total investment in assets that is used to generate those sales.
Sales to Net Working Capital	$= \dfrac{\text{Sales}}{\text{Net Working Capital*}}$	Measures the efficiency of management to use its short-term assets and liabilities to generate revenues
Accounts Payable to Sales =	$\dfrac{\text{Accounts Payable}}{\text{Sales}}$	Measure the extent to which the supplier's money is being used to generate sales. When this ratio is multiplied by 365 days, it reflects the average number of days it takes the company to repay its suppliers.

* Net Working Capital = Current Assets—Current Liabilities
Source: Dun & Bradstreet

Profitability Ratios		
Return on Sales = (Profit Margin)	Net Profit After Taxes / Sales	*Reveals profits earned per dollar of sales and measures the efficiency of the operation.*
Return on Assets =	Net Profit After Taxes / Total Assets	*This is the key indicator of profitability for a firm. It matches net profits with the assets available to earn a return.*
Return on Net Worth = (Return on Equity)	Net Profit after Taxes / Net Worth	*Analyzes the ability of the firm's management to realize an adequate return on the capital invested by the owners of the firm.*

* Net Working Capital = Current Assets—Current Liabilities
Source: Dun & Bradstreet

Fixed income research - yawning?

The attitude of many equity bankers, equity sales and traders, and even some equity research analysts is that fixed income research is the most boring area in any investment bank. Why? Unlike stock analysts, many fixed income analysts do not have clients. If a fixed income analyst issues a report on U.S. Treasury bonds, there is no company calling, fewer surprises, and few salespeople/traders to sing the praises of a good research piece. More importantly, there is often less money to make. While equity analysts often can rise to stardom, those that do in fixed income play second fiddle to the equity guys. However, with the rapid growth in size and complexity of the debt markets in the past decade, interest in fixed income research has substantially increased.

A day in the life of a fixed income analyst

How is the debt analyst different than the equity analyst? As previously mentioned, there is no earnings season driving fixed income as much as there is in equity. Yet quarterly numbers are released and models do need to be updated. Also, corporate bond analysts and high yield analysts do have some seasonal swings. In municipal bond research, emerging markets research, asset-backed research, and government/Treasury research, reports are more evenly spaced and the stress and pressure are often lower. But certain monthly events and surprising news (usually macroeconomic in nature) can spark analysts to stay busy. For example, U.S. Treasury research reports often come out around monthly CPI, PPI and quarterly GDP numbers. In general, interest rate news always impacts bonds, and creates work for analysts to interpret.

The day begins early for the debt research analyst just as it does for the equity analyst. Morning meetings take place around 7:30 a.m. Eastern Time, no matter where you may happen to work. On the West Coast, an analyst must be ready to go at 4:30 in the morning.

The day includes all of the typical work that an equity research analyst does. The analyst is on the phone with buy-side portfolio managers, doing fundamental research, writing reports, tracking bond prices and yield data, and looking for trade ideas to give to the salesforce. Hours tend to resemble the equity analyst, with 12- to 13-hour days the norm, but with less time on the road.

Formulas for Success

Research assistants/associates

To excel initially, research assistants and associates must work hard, learn quickly, and become whizzes at Microsoft Excel and Word. Especially important to research associates are good writing skills, as analysts often hand-off a significant portion of the writing and editing of research reports to the associate. Early on, the biggest mistake a research assistant or associate can make is to mess up the financial models and generally lose sight of the details.

Research is built on a foundation of good models with reasonable assumptions, and research associates must first master that domain. Later on, research assistants and associates must show an ability to handle the phones – answer questions from investors and internal salespeople about the current goings-on at companies they cover, as well as ask smart due diligence questions to company managers in order to generate the next research piece.

Unlike most corporate finance analysts, research assistants/associates can and do rise to the analyst level without an MBA. Some firms promote research assistants to the full-fledged analyst role after one or two years of solid performance, while some hire research associates only for two-year stints, emulating the corporate finance two-year programs. The firms that are less stringent about hiring MBAs full-time for research are more likely to promote internal associates to the analyst position.

Still, the number that makes this jump is a small portion of assistants and associates. Why? Some simply discover that the analyst job is not for them. Many research dropouts move to hedge funds, business school, the buy-side, or institutional sales departments at I-banks. Others simply find that the path to becoming a research analyst nonexistent. Explains one research associate at Morgan Stanley, "A lot of it's demand-driven. If you want to be the head technology analyst, you might have to wait until that person retires or moves to another firm. But sometimes they will add on analysts. Maybe they need a retail analyst to bring I-banking business in. And sometimes a new subsector will turn into a new category."

Research analysts

Newly hired research analysts must start as the associates do—learning, modeling, and working long hours. Beyond the inaugural two years, analysts begin to branch out and become full-fledged analysts, covering their own set of stocks and their own industry segment or sub-segment. Winning respect internally from corporate finance and sales and trading departments may be the first hurdle a new analyst must overcome. This respect comes from detailed research and careful analysis before making assertions about anything. Salespeople can be ruthless when it comes to researchers who make sloppy or unsubstantiated claims. Says one fixed income insider, "There are people who will eat you alive if your analysis is off. They control a huge universe of issues and a huge amount of buyers to make that market liquid, and when you present your analysis you had better be ready. These guys are serious. It's like playing for the San Francisco 49ers; you better be prepared."

Down the road, research analysts—even good ones—are always on somebody's bad side. When the analyst wins respect from the salesperson by turning down a potentially bad IPO, he angers to no end the corporate finance banker who wants to take the company public. When the analyst puts a sell recommendation on a poor stock, the salespeople also cheer, but the company grows angry, sometimes severing all ties with their investment bank. Thus, the best analysts function as diplomats, capable of making clear objective arguments regarding decisions combined with a mix of sweet-talking salespeople and investors.

Do Research Analysts Need MBAs and CFAs?

Although not required, an MBA opens doors in research. Ten years ago, research departments cared little about educational pedigree and a business school education, but today more and more emphasis is being placed on attaining an MBA. Perhaps even more important than earning an MBA for those in research is becoming a **Chartered Financial Analyst**, or CFA. The Association of Investment Management and Research (AIMR) confers this designation on those who pass a series of examinations, which are administered in three stages. They are Levels I, II and III and are given at one-year intervals in May. To become a CFA, one must pass all three levels and also have worked for three years (which usually coincides with the testing period). The program and tests are not easy, and according to the AIMR the pass rates have ranged over the past 10 years:

- **Level I: 48 percent to 62 percent**
- **Level II: 46 percent to 65 percent**
- **Level III: 59 percent to 82 percent**

However, pass rates in recent years have been much lower. In 2006, Level I pass rates were 40%, whereas pass rates for II and III were 48% and 76%, respectively.

The CFA designation lends the analyst respect and credibility to investors and seems more and more a prerequisite to moving up. As one analyst notes, "All things being equal, promotions will go to the analyst with his CFA examinations complete or with his MBA degree." In addition, a candidate interviewing for a research position will stand out by stating a sincere intention to complete the CFA examinations. Unlike an MBA, a CFA certification shows proficiency in understanding a particular area: financial analysis. Therefore, as an analyst publishing investment research with a CFA certification, you are speaking the same language as those on the buy-side who are purchasing your research.

Syndicate:
The Go-betweens

What does the syndicate department at an investment bank do? Syndicate usually sits on the trading floor, but syndicate employees don't trade securities or sell them to clients. They also don't bring in clients for corporate finance and they don't manage market activity like capital markets.

What syndicate does is provide a vital role in placing new equity or debt offerings with buy-siders, and truly aim to find the right offering price that satisfies the company, the salespeople, the investors, and the corporate finance bankers working the deal.

Syndicate and public offerings

In any public offering, syndicate gets involved once the prospectus is filed with the SEC. At that point, syndicate associates begin to contact other investment banks interested in being underwriters in the deal. In a private debt offering, this process is much the same, finding investors to participate in the deal. However, in this section, we'll use an IPO as an example. Before we continue with our discussion of the syndicate's role, we should first understand the difference between managers and underwriters and how fees earned through security offerings are allocated.

Managers

The managers of an IPO get involved from the beginning. These are the I-banks attending all the meetings and generally slaving away to complete the deal. Managers get paid a substantial portion of the total fee—called underwriting discounts and commissions on the cover of a prospectus, and known as the spread in the industry. In an IPO, the spread is usually 7.0 percent, unless the deal is huge, which often means that the offering company can negotiate a slightly lower fee. For a follow-on offering, typical fees start at 5.0 percent, and again, decrease as the deal-size increases. For a debt offering, this fee is usually smaller, in the range of 1-2%.

As discussed previously in this guide, deals typically have between two and five managers. To further confuse the situation, managers are often called managing underwriters, as all managers are underwriters, but not all underwriters are managers. Confused? Keep reading.

Underwriters

The underwriters on the deal are so called because they are the ones assuming liability, though they usually have no shares of stock to sell in the deal. They are not necessarily the I-banks that work intimately on the deal; most underwriters do nothing other than accept any potential liability for lawsuits against the underwriting group. Generally, underwriters are the firms writing the final check to the company, before securities are sold in the market. The term "underwriter" originated from the days of shipping companies, when individuals would sign underneath a ship's name in a ledger, assuming risk for the goods being transported. This process was a way to spread risk (and rewards) across a number of people.

Underwriters are selected by the lead manager in conjunction with the company. This role is often called participating in the syndicate. In a prospectus, you can always find a section entitled "Underwriting," which lists the underwriting group. Anywhere from three to 30 investment banks typically make up the underwriting group in any securities offering. Generally, there are ten to 30 underwriters in an equity offering.

In the underwriting section of an IPO, each participant in the list has a number of shares associated with its name. While underwriting sections list quite a few investment banks and shares next to each bank, it is important to realize that these banks do not sell shares. Neither do they have anything to do with how the shares in the deal are allocated to investors. They merely assume the percentage of liability indicated by the percentage of deal shares listed in the prospectus. To take on such liability, underwriters are paid a small fee, depending on their level of underwriting involvement (i.e., the number of shares next to their name). The managers in the deal will account for the liability of approximately 50 to 70 percent of the shares, while the underwriters account for the rest.

The Economics of a Deal

Suppose there are three managers in an IPO transaction for ABC Corporation. Say the deal is $200 million in size. And let's say that this $200 million is accounted for because the deal is priced at $20 per share and the company is offering 10 million shares to the public. With a 7.0 percent spread (the deal fee percent typical in IPOs), we come up with a whopping $14 million fee.

How is the $14 million divided up? Each department is actually allocated a piece of the deal before the firms divide their shares. First, corporate finance (the bankers working the deal) grabs 20 percent of the fee. So, in our example, $2.8 million (20 percent of $14 million) is split among the three managers' corporate finance departments. Then the salespeople from the managing group take their share—a whooping 60 percent of the spread, totaling $8.4 million. Again, this $8.4 million is divided by the few managers in the deal.

This 20/60 split is typical for almost any deal. The last portion of the spread goes to the syndicate group (a.k.a. the underwriters) and is appropriately called the underwriting fee. However, expenses for the deal are taken out of the underwriting fee, so it never amounts to a full 20 percent of the spread. Suppose that this deal had 20 underwriters. The underwriting section in the prospectus might look like:

Underwriter	# of shares
I-Bank 1 (the lead manager)	7,000,000
I-Bank 2 (a co-manager)	4,000,000
I-Bank 3 (a co-manager)	4,000,000
I-Bank 4	294,118
I-Bank 5	294,118
• • • •	• • • •
I-Bank 20	294,118
TOTAL	20,000,000

The total number of shares accounted for by each underwriter (the number of shares each underwriter assumes liability for) adds up to the total number of shares sold in the transaction. Note that the managers or underwriting managers take the biggest chunk of the liability. (In this case, each manager would pay 25 percent of damages from a lawsuit, as 5,000,000 shares represent 25 percent of the 20,000,000-share offering.)

If we return to our example, we see that after the sales and corporate finance managers are paid, the last 20 percent comes out to $2.8 million. This is quite a bit of money. However, the way deals work, expenses are netted against the underwriting fee. Flights to the company, lawyers, roadshow expenses, etc., all add up to a lot of money and are taken out of the underwriting fee. Why? Nobody exactly knows why this is the practice, except that it doesn't seem quite fair to

Visit the Vault Finance Career Channel at **www.vault.com/finance** – with
insider firm profiles, message boards, the Vault Finance Job Board and more.

VAULT CAREER LIBRARY   **157**

have the syndicate receive as much as the bankers—who put in countless weekends and hours putting together a deal.

Let's pretend that deal expenses totaled $1.8 million, leaving

$2.8 million Underwriting Fees
- $1.8 million Expenses
Underwriting Profit $1.0 million

Therefore, the lead manager gets 35 percent of the underwriting profit (7,000,000 shares divided by the total 20,000,000 = 35 percent). The two co-managers each receive 20 percent of the underwriting profit (4,000,000 divided by 20,000,000) and each underwriter receives approximately 1.47 percent of the underwriting profit (294,118 divided by 20,000,000). Therefore the lead manager gets $350,000 of the underwriting profit, the co-managers each get $200,000, and the other underwriters each get approximately $14,706. Not bad for doing practically nothing but taking on minimal risk.

Why the long diversion into the mechanics of what an underwriter is and how much they are paid? Because this is what syndicate spends considerable time doing.

Syndicate professionals:

- Make sure their banks are included in the underwriting of other deals
- Put together the underwriting group in deals the I-bank is managing
- Allocate stock to the various buy-side firms indicating interest in deal
- Determine the final offering price of various offerings

What is involved on a day-to-day basis? Quite a bit of phone time and quite of bit of dealing with the book.

The book

As mentioned earlier, the "**book**" is a listing of all investors who have indicated interest in buying stock in an offering. Investors place orders by telling their respective salesperson at the investment bank or by calling the syndicate department of the lead manager. Only the lead manager maintains (or carries) the book in a deal.

Orders can come in one of two forms – either an order for a specified number of shares at any price, or for a specified number of shares up to a specified price. Most buy-siders indicate a price range of some kind. Often, large institutions come in with a "10 percent order." That is the goal of the managers, and means that the investor wants to buy 10 percent of the shares in the deal.

In terms of timing, the book comes together during the roadshow, as investors meet the company's management team. Adding to the excitement, many investors wait until the day or two prior to pricing to call in their order. Thus, a manager may not know if they can sell the deal until the very last minute. The day before the securities begin to trade, syndicate looks at the book and calls each potential buyer one last time. It is important to ferret out which money managers are serious about owning the stock/bonds over the long haul. Those that don't are called flippers. Why would a money manager choose this strategy? Because in a good market, getting shares in the offering is often a sure way to make money, as stocks usually jump up a few percentage points at the opening bell. However, **flippers** are the bane of successful offerings. Institutional money managers who buy into public deals just to sell their shares on the first day only cause the stock to immediately trade down. Syndicate teams become wary of habitual flippers and make sure to allocate few shares to them, only if need be.

Pricing and allocation

How does syndicate price a stock? Simple – by supply and demand. There are a fixed number of shares or bonds in a public deal available, and buyers indicate exactly how many shares and at what price they are willing to purchase the securities. The problem is that most deals are **oversubscribed**; i.e., there are more shares demanded than available for sale. Therefore, syndicate must determine how many shares to allocate to each buyer. To add to the headache, because investors know that every successful deal is oversubscribed, they inflate their actual share indications. So, a 10 percent order may in fact mean that the money manager actually wants something like 2 or 3 percent of the deal. The irony, then, is that any money manager that actually got as many shares as she asked for would immediately cancel her order, realizing that the deal was a "dog."

In the end, a combination of syndicate's experience with investors and their instincts about buyers tells them how many shares to give to each buy-sider. Syndicate tries to avoid flippers, but can never entirely do so.

Visit the Vault Finance Career Channel at **www.vault.com/finance** – with insider firm profiles, message boards, the Vault Finance Job Board and more.

V/\ULT CAREER LIBRARY   **159**

After the book is set, syndicate calls the offering company to report the details. This "**pricing call**," as it is called, occurs immediately after the roadshow ends and the day before the stock begins trading in the market. Pricing calls sometimes results in yelling, cursing and swearing from the management teams of companies going public. Remember that in IPOs, the call is telling founders of companies what their firm is worth—reactions sometimes border on the extreme. If a deal is not hot (as most are not), then the given price may be disappointing to the company. "How can my company not be the greatest thing the market has ever seen?" CEOs often think.

Also, company managers often mistakenly believe that the pricing call is some sort of negotiation, and fire back with higher prices. However, only on rare occasions can the CEO influence the final price – and even then only a little. Their negotiating strength stems from the fact that they can walk away from a deal. Managers will then be out months of work and a lot of money (deal expenses can be very high). An untold number of deals have been shelved because the company has insisted on another 50 cents on the offered share price, and the syndicate department has told management that it simply is not feasible. It may sound like a pittance, but on a 20 million share deal, 50 cents per share is a whopping $10 million in proceeds to the company (less underwriting fees).

Politicians

Because of this tension over the offering price, senior syndicate professionals must be able to handle difficult and delicate situations. But it's not just company management that must be handled with care. During a deal, syndicate must also deal with the salesforce, other underwriters, and buy-siders. Similar to the research analyst, the syndicate professional often finds that diplomacy is one of the most critical elements to success. Successful syndicate pros can read between the lines and figure out the real intentions of buy-siders (are they flippers or are they committed to the offering, do they really want 10 percent of the offering, etc.). Also, good syndicate associates are proficient at schmoozing with other investment banks and garnering underwriting business (when the syndicate department is not representing the manager).

It's still a bank, not a cocktail party

Although syndicate professionals must have people skills, a knack for number-crunching and market knowledge are also important. Offerings involve many buy orders at various prices and for various levels of stock. Syndicate must allocate down from the biggest institutional investors to the smallest retail client (if retail clients are allowed to get shares in the deal). And pricing is quite a mix of art and science. Judging market momentum, deal interest and company egos can be trying indeed.

Who works in syndicate?

As for the players in syndicate, some have MBAs, and some don't. Some worked their way up, and some were hired directly into an associate syndicate position. The payoffs in syndicate can be excellent for top dogs, as the most advanced syndicate pros often deal directly with clients (management teams of companies doing an offering), handle pricing calls, and talk to the biggest investors. They essentially become salespeople themselves, touting the firm, their expertise in placing stock or bonds, and their track record. Occasionally, syndicate MDs will attend an important deal pitch to potential clients, especially if he or she is a good talker. At the same time, some syndicate professionals move into sales or other areas, often in order to get away from the endless politicking involved with working in the syndicate department.

Beginners in the syndicate department help put together the book, schedule roadshow meetings and work their way up to dealing with investors, other I-banks, and internal sales. Because syndicate requires far fewer people than other areas in the bank, fewer job openings are to be found. Rarely does a firm recruit on college campuses for syndicate jobs—instead, firms generally hire from within the industry or from within the firm.

How is capital markets different from syndicate?

This is a fundamentally important distinction. Both syndicate and capital markets professionals understand everything in their markets. Both functions act as the liaison between the markets and deal teams. Furthermore, both advise clients on transactions. Confused? Keep reading.

The fundamental difference between capital markets and syndicate is that the syndicate teams generally only work with deal teams when a deal is "mandated" (legal documents, such as commitment and fee letters have been executed) and about to be priced in the market. After a transaction has been priced, it becomes a "comp" for future deal teams and is off the syndicate's desk. On the other hand, capital markets works with deal teams all throughout the process, from pitch phase to execution, to close.

Ultimately, syndicate professionals are entirely responsible for the pricing phase and capital markets professionals are responsible for the rest.

How are private debt issuances different from IPOs?

With over a $1.4 trillion of annual new issuance volume, the syndicated loan market has its own set of issuance rules. Although many processes and procedures remain the same as an IPO (underwriting, circling the book, allocations), many things are different. The process usually depends on the nature of the loan. As a rule of thumb, loans originated for a transaction (LBO, Recap, Restructuring) are underwritten, whereas loans originated for backup reasons (Commercial Paper backstop, Working Capital) are usually arranged on a best-efforts basis. The fundamental difference is that an underwritten transaction guarantees a company a certain amount of funds, whereas a best-efforts deal does not.

Depending on the size of the loan package, underwriting or arranging could involve either a sole bank or a group of banks, often called bookrunners or arrangers. In the largest of financings, this number usually does not exceed three arrangers (as league table agencies have limits). Thus, "sole-books" refers to a deal with one bookrunner, whereas "joint-books" refers to a deal with either two or three bookrunners. As with IPO and Bond offerings, the lead-left bookrunner does the majority of the work ("lead-left" refers to the bank that is on the far left of the offering memorandum, thus signifying its leadership of the deal).

Depending on the size of the facility, the arrangers reach out to banks and institutional investors in order to build a book during what is known as a "commitment period". Much like the IPO process, investors come back to the arrangers either their commitments to the deal. To signify their levels of commitment to the deal, titles are usually given out, such as "agent," "co-agent," and "participant." The aggregate levels of commitment will determine whether or not a deal is oversubscribed or not. If an underwritten deal fails to reach the target level of the arranger(s), then they are responsible for the remaining balance (note that in best-efforts, the arrangers are not on the hook for the remaining cash).

Much like with an IPO offering, loan spreads may be adjusted throughout the offering process, depending on investor interest. The spread may be changed, the size of the loan may be increased or decreased, call protection may be added or removed, and even the offer price might be changed in order to adjust for yield (although, like bonds, most loans are issued at "par" or 100).

APPENDIX

Glossary

8-K: A report filed with the SEC by a public company to update investors of any material event

10-K: An annual set of audited financial statements of a public company filed with the SEC. The 10-K includes a balance sheet, cash flow statement, and income statement, as well as an explanation of the company's performance (usually referred to as Management's Discussion and Analysis). It is audited by an accounting firm before being registered.

10-Q: A set of quarterly financial statements of a public company filed with the SEC. The 10-Q includes a balance sheet, cash flow statement, and income statement, among other things. As the fourth quarter's performance is captured in the 10-K, public companies must only file 3 of these per year.

Annual report: A combination of financial statements, management discussion and analysis, and graphs and charts provided annually to investors; they're required for companies traded publicly in the U.S.

Arranger: An institution involved in leading a financing transaction. Also commonly referred to as a "bookrunner."

Asset management: Also known as investment management. Money managers at investment management firms and investment banks take money given to them by pension funds and individual investors and invest it. For wealthy individuals (private clients), the investment bank will set up an individual account and manage the account; for the less well-endowed, the bank will offer mutual funds. Asset managers are compensated primarily by taking a percentage each year from the total assets managed. (They may also charge an upfront load, or commission, of a few percent of the initial money invested.)

Audit: An examination of transactions and financial statements made in accordance with generally accepted auditing standards.

Auditor: A person who examines the information used by managers to prepare the financial statements and attests to the credibility of those statements.

Balance Sheet: One of the three main financial statements (Balance Sheet, Cash Flow Statement, Income Statement), the balance sheet is a snapshot in time of a company's assets, liabilities, and owner's equity. Public companies must issue these statements on a quarterly basis in their 10-Qs and at the end of their fiscal year in a 10-K.

Basis points (bps): The general way spreads are measured in finance. 100 basis points = 1 percent

Bilateral loan: A loan between two parties; the company and a sole lender. Bilateral loans are common for loans less than $10MM.

Bloomberg: A computer terminal most commonly found on the desks of sales people and traders, providing current and historical market information, as well as e-mail and instant messaging services.

Bookrunner: The firm or firms leading a financing transaction. "Sole-books" refers to a deal with only one leading institution, whereas "joint-books" refers to a deal with 2 or more institutions. The term "bookrunner" is also synonymous with "arranger."

Bond spreads: The difference between the yield of a corporate bond and a U.S. Treasury security of similar time to maturity.

Bulge bracket: The largest and most prestigious firms on Wall Street (including Citibank, Credit Suisse, Deutsche Bank, Goldman Sachs, JPMorgan, Lehman Brothers, Morgan Stanley, and Merrill Lynch.

Buy-side: The clients of investment banks (mutual funds, pension funds) who buy the stocks, bonds and securities sold by the banks. (The investment banks that sell these products to investors are known as the sell-side.)

Call protection: A mechanism used to entice investors to purchase debt securities, whereby a company must pay a premium to repurchase its debt during a specified period of time. Call protection is usually stated in 1 percent and one year increments. For example, call protection of "102/101" would mean that a company has the right to repurchase its debt for 102 cents on the dollar in the first year, 101 cents in the second year, and par thereafter. The term "NC" refers to a no-call period, where a company is restricted from repurchasing its debt for a certain period of time, usually a year.

Capital Expenditure: A major expenditure by a company on a physical asset in order to operate the business on a day to day basis. CapEx might include purchasing a building, machinery, or even land. Investment bankers make a distinction between growth and maintenance CapEx, when evaluating the performance of a company.

Capital Structure: This refers to the composition of a company's debt and equity, including stock, bonds, and loans.

Cash flow statement: One of the three main financial statements (Balance Sheet, Cash Flow Statement, Income Statement), the cash flow statement summarizes the cash sources and uses of a company over a period of a year. Public companies must issue these statements on a quarterly basis in their 10-Qs and at the end of their fiscal year in a 10-K.

Certified public accountant (CPA): In the United States, a person earns this designation through a combination of education, qualifying experience and by passing a national written examination.

Chapter 7: The portion of the bankruptcy code that results in the liquidation of a company's assets in order to pay off outstanding financial obligations.

Chapter 11: The portion of the bankruptcy code that allows a company to operate under the bankruptcy court's supervision for an indefinite period of time, generally resulting in a corporate restructuring with the assistance of an investment bank.

Chartered Financial Analyst (CFA): A designation given to professionals who complete a multi-part exam designed to test accounting and investment knowledge and professional ethics.

Chinese Wall: The separation between public and private sections of an investment bank, including sales, trading & research from corporate finance. Many banks even have physical barriers and/or e-mail restrictions to support this effort.

Collateralized Debt Obligation (CDO): A type of structured product or derivative, comprised of multiple tranches of debt of different companies.. These debt tranches typically take the form of loans or bonds.

Commercial bank: A bank that lends, rather than raises, money. For example, if a company wants $30 million to open a new production plant, it can approach a commercial bank for a loan.

Commercial paper: Short-term corporate debt, typically maturing in nine months or less.

Commitment letter: A document that outlines the terms of a loan a commercial bank gives a client. For example, in a $5 billion transaction underwritten by three banks, the commitment letter would outline the amount each bank would underwrite and the corresponding terms.

Commodities: Assets (usually agricultural products or metals) that are generally interchangeable with one another and therefore share a common price. For example, corn, wheat and rubber generally trade at one price on commodity markets worldwide.

Common stock: Also called common equity, common stock represents an ownership interest in a company. (As opposed to preferred stock, see below.) The vast majority of stock traded in the markets today is common, as common stock enables investors to vote on company matters. An individual who owns at least 51 percent of a company's stocks controls the company's decisions and can appoint anyone he/she wishes to the board of directors or to the management team.

Comparable company analysis (Comps): The primary tool of the corporate finance analyst. Comps include a list of financial data, valuation data and ratio data on a set of companies in an industry. Comps are used to value private companies or better understand a how the market values an industry or particular player in the industry.

Consumer Price Index (CPI): The CPI measures the percentage increase in a standard basket of goods and services. The CPI is a measure of inflation for consumers.

Convertible bonds: Bonds that can be converted into a specified number of shares of stock.

Credit Agreement: The physical document that outlines the terms and provisions of a syndicated loan. The credit agreement is signed both by investors and the company. Credit agreements can sometimes be found in a company's 10-K, although they are not required.

Credit Cycle: The general market cycle of company defaults (companies that declare bankruptcy due to lack of an ability to meet their financial obligations). Credit cycles tend to be at their best (their lowest) during periods of low interest rates and general overall market health. Credit cycles generally occur in five- to seven-year periods.

Crossover-credit: This refers to a company that is rated investment grade by one rating agency and leveraged by another.

Derivatives: An asset whose value is derived from the price of another asset. Examples include call options, put options, CDOs, futures and interest-rate swaps.

Debtor in Possession (DIP): A DIP loan is a loan made to a company currently operating in Chapter 11 bankruptcy. DIP refers to the nature of the loan, whereby the company retains possession of the assets for which investors have a claim.

Discount rate: A widely followed short-term interest rate set by the Federal Reserve to cause market interest rates to rise or fall, thereby spurring the U.S. economy to grow more quickly or less quickly. More specifically, the discount rate is the rate at which federal banks lend money to each other on overnight loans. Today, the discount rate can be directly moved by the Fed, but largely maintains a symbolic role.

Discounted Cash Flow: Used in NPV analysis, the discounted cash flow method takes into account the future cash flows of a project or company, discounted back to the present using the firm's cost of capital. DCF is most likely the most important concept a corporate finance analyst must master in order to be successful. It is at the very core of most financial modeling.

Dividend: A payment by a company to shareholders of its stock, usually as a way to distribute profits.

EBITDA: Earnings Before Interest, Taxes, Depreciation, and Amortization. EBITDA is generally used as a proxy for a company' cash flow. Although not as useful in equity investing, EBITDA (not Net Income) is the most important financial term in debt investing.

Equity: In short, stock. Equity means ownership in a company that is usually represented by stock, whether public or private.

ERISA: Employee Retirement Income Security Act of 1974. The federal law that sets most pension plan requirements.

ETF: Exchange-traded Fund. ETFs are listed as individual securities in the equity markets and are used to replicate an index or a portfolio of stocks.

The Fed: The Federal Reserve, which gently (or sometimes roughly), manages the country's economy by setting interest rates. The current chairman of the Fed is Ben Bernanke and the former chairman was Alan Greenspan.

Federal funds rate: The rate domestic banks charge one another on overnight loans to meet Federal Reserve requirements. This rate tracks very closely to the discount rate, but is usually slightly higher.

Financial accounting: The field of accounting that serves external decision makers, such as stockholders, suppliers, banks and government agencies.

Financial Accounting Standards Board (FASB): A private-sector body that determines generally accepted accounting principles in the United States.

Financial Sponsor: A general term used to refer to a firm that completes a financial transaction, such as an LBO, on behalf of another company. Financial sponsors are also known as private equity firms.

Fixed income: Bonds and other securities that earn a fixed rate of return. Bonds are typically issued by governments, corporations and municipalities.

Free Cash Flow: The measure of cash that a company has left over after paying for its existing operations. FCF is generally calculated as Operating Income minus Maintenance CapEx and Dividends.

Generally Accepted Accounting Principles (GAAP): The broad concepts or guidelines and detailed practices in accounting, including all conventions, rules and procedures that make up accepted accounting practices.

Glass-Steagall Act: Part of the legislation passed in 1933 during the Great Depression designed to help prevent future bank failure—the establishment of the F.D.I.C. was also part of this movement. The Glass-Steagall Act split America's investment-banking (issuing and trading securities) operations from commercial banking (lending). For example, JPMorgan was forced to spin off its securities unit as Morgan Stanley. The act was gradually weakened throughout the 1990s. In 1999 Glass-Steagall was effectively repealed by the Graham-Leach-Bliley Act.

Graham-Leach-Bliley Act: Also known as the Financial Services Modernization Act of 1999. Essentially repealed many of the restrictions of the Glass-Steagall Act and made possible the current trend of consolidation in the financial services industry. Allows commercial banks, investment banks and insurance companies to affiliate under a holding company structure.

Greenshoe option: An IPO over-allotment option that allows for underwriters to issue up to 15% more of the underlying firm's stock, in the event the offering is well received by investors. "Greenshoe" refers to the Green Shoe Company, which was the first to exercise such an option.

Growth stock: Industry leaders that investors and analysts believe will continue to prosper and exceed expectations. These companies have above average revenue and earnings growth and their stocks trade at high price-to-earnings and price-to-book ratios. Technology and telecommunications companies such as Microsoft and Cisco are good examples of traditional growth stocks.

Hedge: To balance a position in the market in order to reduce risk. Hedges work like insurance: a small position pays off large amounts with a slight move in the market.

Hedge fund: An investment partnership, similar to a mutual fund, made up of wealthy investors. In comparison to most investment vehicles, hedge funds are loosely regulated, allowing them to take more risks with their investments.

High-grade corporate bond: A corporate bond with a rating above BB^+. Also called investment grade debt.

High-yield debt (a.k.a. Junk bonds): Corporate bonds that pay high interest rates (to compensate investors for high risk of default). Credit rating agencies such as Standard & Poor's rate a company's (or a municipality's) bonds based on default risk. Junk bonds rate at or below BB+.

Income statement: One of the three main financial statements (Balance Sheet, Cash Flow Statement, Income Statement), the income statement summarizes the sales and costs of a company's operations over the period of a year. Public companies must issue these statements on a quarterly basis in their 10-Qs and at the end of their fiscal year in a 10-K.

Initial public offering (IPO): The dream of just about every entrepreneur, the IPO marks the first time a company issues stock to the public. Going public means more than raising money for the company: by agreeing to take on public shareholders, a company enters a whole world of required SEC filings and quarterly revenue and earnings reports, not to mention possible shareholder lawsuits.

Institutional clients or investors: Large investors, such as hedge funds, pension funds, or municipalities (as opposed to retail investors or individual investors).

Interest Coverage ratio: A financial ratio used by investors to assess a company's ability to pay the interest on its debt. Usually measured as EBITDA/Interest Expense, often a fixed number (or a schedule of numbers) is structured into loan contracts. Investors tend to focus very heavily on both the coverage and leverage ratios of a company before investing in its debt.

Visit the Vault Finance Career Channel at **www.vault.com/finance** – with insider firm profiles, message boards, the Vault Finance Job Board and more.

V/\ULT CAREER LIBRARY   **171**

Investment grade: This refers to companies or debt securities with a BBB- or better S&P rating (or Baa3 or better Moody's rating).

Lead manager: The primary investment bank managing a securities offering. (An investment bank may share this responsibility with one or more co-managers.)

League tables: Tables that rank investment banks based on volume in numerous categories, such as stocks, bonds, high yield debt, convertible debt, syndicated loans, etc. High rankings in league tables are key selling points used by investment banks when trying to land a client. Thomson Financial is the most widely used independent source of league tables.

Leverage Ratio: A financial ratio used by investors to assess a company's debt obligations in relation to its cash flow. Usually measured as Total Debt/EBITDA, often a fixed number (or a schedule of numbers) is structured into loan contracts. Investors tend to focus very heavily on both the coverage and leverage ratios of a company before investing in its debt.

Leveraged: This refers to companies or debt securities with a BB+ or lower S&P rating (or Ba1 or lower Moody's rating).

Leveraged buyout (LBO): The buyout of a company with borrowed money, often using that company's own assets as collateral. LBOs were the order of the day in the heady 1980s, when successful LBO firms such as Kohlberg Kravis Roberts made a practice of buying up companies, restructuring them and then reselling them or taking them public at a significant profit. Today, volume to the LBO market has returned again to record levels with three of the largest four LBOs of all time having been accomplished in the past year.

LIBOR: London Interbank Offered Rate. The risk-free rate by which banks lend to one another in London. Syndicated loans are priced with spreads above LIBOR. Very similar to the Federal Funds rate.

The Long Bond: The 30-year U.S. Treasury bond. Treasury bonds are used as the starting point for pricing many other bonds, because Treasury bonds are assumed to have zero credit risk taking into account factors such as inflation. For example, a company will issue a bond that trades "40 over Treasuries." The "40" refers to 40 basis points (100 basis points = 1 percentage point).

LTM: Last Twelve Months. When analyzing companies, investors not only focus on quarterly results, but also on the performance of the company over the Last Twelve Months. Often times, company 10-Q's will include quarterly results, as well as LTM performance.

Mandate: When a firm is officially offered a transaction by a client, this is called "winning the mandate." Although exciting, this typically signifies the end of the pitch phase and the beginning of the long and arduous deal execution process.

Making markets: A function performed by investment banks to provide liquidity for their clients in a particular security, often for a security that the investment bank has underwritten. (In others words, the investment bank stands willing to buy the security, if necessary, when the investor later decides to sell it.)

Market capitalization (market cap): The total value of a company in the stock market (total shares outstanding multiplied by price per share).

Merchant banking: The department within an investment bank that invests the firm's own money in other companies. Analogous to a private equity arm.

Money market securities: This term is generally used to represent the market for securities maturing within one year. These include short-term CDs, repurchase agreements and commercial paper (low-risk corporate issues), among others. These are low risk, short-term securities that have yields similar to Treasuries.

Mortgage-backed bonds: Bonds collateralized by a pool of mortgages. Interest and principal payments are based on the individual homeowners making their mortgage payments. The more diverse the pool of mortgages backing the bond, the less risky they are.

Municipal bonds (Munis): Bonds issued by local and state governments, a.k.a. municipalities. Municipal bonds are structured as tax-free for the investor, which means investors in munis earn interest payments without having to pay federal taxes. Sometimes investors are exempt from state and local taxes, too. Consequently, municipalities can pay lower interest rates on muni bonds than other bonds of similar risk.

Mutual fund: An investment vehicle that collects funds from investors (both individual and institutional) and invests in a variety of securities, including stocks and bonds. Mutual funds make money by charging a percentage of assets in the fund.

Net Present Value: The method by which a company compares whether or not a project will be profitable, by using DCF. NPV analysis takes into account the cost and benefits of a project, using Time Value of Money, as well as a firm's opportunity cost. The basic rule of thumb is that if a project is NPV positive, it should be accepted. NPV is also at the very core of most financial modeling by investment bankers.

Offering Memorandum: Also referred to as an Information Memorandum, the OM is a marketing document prepared by an investment bank for a loan offering. The OM generally contains transaction, competitor, financial, management, and investment risk information. OMs are circulated to investors in order to educate them about the company, before investing in the company's securities. OMs are similar in nature to a bond prospectus.

P/E ratio: The price-to-earnings ratio. This is the ratio of a company's stock price to its earnings-per-share. The higher the P/E ratio, the more expensive a stock is (and the faster investors believe the company will grow). Stocks in fast-growing industries tend to have higher P/E ratios.

Par: In trading, this refers to when a debt securing is trading at 100. Most loans and bonds are issued at par. If they are issued at a discount, this is anything less than par. Conversely, a premium is anything more than par. When trading at par, the yield of the security can be inferred to be the same as its coupon. When trading below par, the security has a higher implied yield, as securities are eventually redeemed at par. Therefore, a 5 percent bond trading at 98 actually has more than a 5 percent yield, since it will eventually be repurchased at 100. Thus, the investor will get this 2 point increase, as well as the 5 percent coupon.

Pari Passu: Latin for "without partiality," this refers to when two or more instruments share the same seniority in a company's capital structure.

Passive investor: Relies on diversification to match the performance of a stock market index (e.g., the S&P 500 Index or the the Wilshire 4500 Completion Index). Because a passive portfolio strategy involves matching an index, this strategy is commonly referred to as indexing.

PIB: Public Information Book. Generally prepared by analysts, PIBs are a compilation of all public information that exists for a company, including public financials, press releases, and analyst reports. Before the due-diligence phase, corporate finance teams will usually read through these to get a better idea of the company's recent activities and performance.

Pit traders: Traders who are positioned on the floor of stock and commodity exchanges (as opposed to floor traders, situated in investment bank offices).

Pitchbook: The book of exhibits, graphs and initial recommendations presented by bankers to prospective clients when trying to land an engagement.

Prime rate: The base rate U.S. banks use to price loans for their best customers.

Private accountants. Accountants who work for businesses, as well as government agencies, and other non-profit organizations.

Private Equity: Also called "financial sponsors", this term refers to the group of investment firms that raise cash from investors to purchase public and private companies through LBOs. Big name firms include: Bain Capital, Blackstone, Carlyle, Hicks, Muse, Tate & Furst (recently renamed HM Capital), JPMorgan Partners, KKR, Madison Dearborn, Texas Pacific Group, and Thomas H. Lee.

Producer Price Index: The PPI measures the percentage increase in a standard basket of goods and services. PPI is a measure of inflation for producers and manufacturers.

Proprietary trading: Trading of the firm's own assets (as opposed to trading client assets). Also occasionally referred to as principal investing.

Prospectus: A report issued by a company (filed with and approved by the SEC) that wishes to sell securities to investors. Distributed to prospective investors, the prospectus discloses the company's financial position, business description and risk factors.

Public accountants. Accountants who offer services to the general public on a fee basis including auditing, tax work and management consulting.

Purchase Price Multiple: The ratio measuring a firm's LBO purchase price in comparison to its EBITDA. Purchase price multiples are crucial for private equity firms valuing potential targets.

Rating Agency Presentation (RAP): The deck of slides used by investment banks when presenting a security for rating by one of the major rating agencies: Moody's or S&P.

Recapitalization: A transaction where a company's capital structure is changed, by issuing one security for another. Recapitalizations often involve the repurchase of shares by the issuance of debt or the replacement of existing debt with a new type and/or different-sized tranche. Often times, a recapitalization can be done to fend off a hostile takeover, by issuing debt for the company to repurchase existing equity shares.

Request for proposal (RFP): Statement issued by institutions (i.e., pension funds or corporate retirement plans) when they are looking to hire a new investment manager. RFPs typically detail the style of money management required and the types of credentials needed.

Retail clients: Individual investors (as opposed to institutional clients).

Return on equity: The ratio of a firm's profits to the value of its equity. Return on equity, or ROE, is a commonly used measure of how well an investment bank is doing, because it measures how efficiently and profitably the firm is using its capital.

Roadshow: The series of presentations to investors that a company undergoing an IPO usually gives in the weeks preceding the offering. Here's how it works: The company and its investment bank will travel to major cities throughout the country. In each city, the company's top executives make a presentation to analysts, mutual fund managers and other attendees, while answering questions.

S-1: A type of legal document filed with the SEC for a private company aiming to go public. The S-1 is almost identical to the prospectus sent to potential investors. The SEC must approve the S-1 before the stock can be sold to investors.

S-2: A type of legal document filed with the SEC for a public company looking to sell additional shares in the market. The S-2 is almost identical to the prospectus sent to potential investors. The SEC must approve the S-2 before the stock is sold.

Sales memo: Short reports written by the corporate finance bankers and distributed to the bank's salespeople. The sales memo provides salespeople with points to emphasize when marketing to investors the stocks and bonds the firm is underwriting.

Securities and Exchange Commission (SEC): A federal agency that, like the Glass-Steagall Act, was established as a result of the stock market crash of 1929 and the ensuing depression. The SEC monitors disclosure of financial information to stockholders and protects against fraud. Publicly traded securities must be approved by the SEC prior to trading.

Secured Debt: Debt that is secured by the assets of the firm is referred to as secured debt. Although usually coming in the form of loans, secured debt can also take the form of bonds. If a company is liquidated, those investors in the firm's secured debt are paid out first and foremost with the proceeds from the sale of the firm's assets. Secured debt is almost entirely classified as "senior debt."

Sell-side: Investment banks and other firms that sell securities to investors, both retail and institutional. Naturally, investors purchasing these securities are on the buy-side.

Senior Debt: Most often in the form of loans or bonds, this refers to debt that has repayment priority in the event of bankruptcy. "Senior" also refers to the place of the debt in the firm's capital structure in comparison to other instruments of the same type. If a firm is liquidated, its senior debt is paid out before its junior debt. Therefore, junior debt usually must compensate investors with higher yield from spreads for this increased risk.

Short-term debt: A bond that matures in nine months or less. Also called commercial paper.

Specialty firm: An investment management firm that focus on one type of style, product or client type.

Syndicate: A group of investment banks that together will underwrite a particular stock or debt offering. Usually the lead manager will underwrite the bulk of a deal, while other members of the syndicate will each underwrite a small portion.

Syndicated Loan: This refers to a type of loan provided to a company by a group of lenders (investment banks and/or institutions).

T-Bill Yields: The yield or internal rate of return an investor would receive at any given moment on a 90-120 government treasury bill.

Tax-exempt bonds: Municipal bonds (also known as munis). Munis are free from federal taxes and, sometimes, state and local taxes.

Tombstone: Usually found in pitchbooks, these are logos and details from past successful deals done by an investment bank. Often times for hallmark transactions, these same details will be placed on a notable object and distributed to the company and bankers, to serve as a memento of a deal. For example, a high-yield bond for a sporting equipment manufacturer might be commemorated with actual baseball bats or footballs, inscribed with transaction information.

Treasury securities: Securities issued by the U.S. government. These are divided into Treasury Bills (maturity of up to two years), Treasury Notes (from two years to 10 years maturity), and Treasury Bonds (10 years to 30 years). As they are government guaranteed, treasuries are often considered risk-free. In fact, while U.S. Treasuries have no default risk, they do have interest rate risk; if rates increase, then the price of U.S. Treasuries will decrease.

Treasury stock: Common stock that is owned by the company but not outstanding, with the intent either to be reissued at a later date, or retired. It is not included in the calculations of financial ratios, such as P/E or EPS, but is included in the company's financial statements.

Underwrite: The function performed by investment banks when they help companies issue securities to investors. Technically, the investment bank buys the securities from the company and immediately resells the securities to investors for a slightly higher price, making money on the spread.

Value stock: Well-established, high dividend paying companies with low price to earnings and price to book ratios. Essentially, they are "diamonds in the rough" that typically have undervalued assets and earnings potential.

Classic value stocks include oil companies like ExxonMobil and banks such as BankAmerica or JPMorgan Chase.

Yield: The annual return on investment. A high yield bond, for example, pays a high rate of interest

Recommended Reading

Suggested Texts

Brandt, Richard and Weisel, Thomas. *Capital Instincts: Life as an Entrepreneur, Financier, and Athlete.* Hoboken, NJ: John Wiley & Sons, 2003

Burrough, Bryan and Helyar, John. *Barbarians at the Gate: The Fall of RJR Nabisco.* New York: Harper & Row, 1990.

Chernow, Ron, *The House of Morgan: An American Banking Dynasty and the Rise of Modern Finance.* New York: Atlantic Monthly Press, 1990.

Endlich, Lisa. *Goldman Sachs: The Culture of Success.* New York: Alfred A. Knopf, 1999.

Gordon, John Steele, *The Great Game: The Emergence of Wall Street As a World Power.* 1653-2000. New York: Scribner, 1999.

Josephson, Matthew, *The Robber Barons.* New York: Harcourt, Brace, and Company, 1962.

Lewis, Michael. *Liar's Poker.* New York: Norton, 1989.

Lewis, Michael. *The Money Culture.* New York: W. W. Norton, 1991.

Lowenstein, Roger. *When Genius Failed: The Rise and Fall of Long-Term Capital Management.* New York: Random House, 2000

Rolfe, John and Traub, Peter. *Monkey Business: Swinging Through the Wall Street Jungle.* New York: Warner Books, 2000.

Stewart, James Brewer. *Den of Thieves.* New York: Simon and Schuster, 1991.

Suggested Periodicals

• *American Banker*	• *Fortune*
• *Business Week*	• *Institutional Investor*
• *The Deal*	• *Investment Dealers' Digest*
• *The Economist*	• *Investor's Business Daily*
• *Forbes*	• *The Wall Street Journal*

About the Authors

Tom Lott, born in Dallas, Texas, graduated from Vanderbilt University in 1993. He started in the investment banking business upon graduation, joining Raymond James & Associates, an investment bank in St. Petersburg, Florida. His work experience includes a brief stint in research and four years in corporate finance. He obtained his MBA from the J.L. Kellogg Graduate School of Management (Northwestern), where he served as chairman of the investments club. He now works in fixed income trading at Merrill Lynch in New York City.

Derek Loosvelt is a graduate of the Wharton School at the University of Pennsylvania. He's a Brooklyn-based writer and editor and has worked for Brill's Content and Inside.com. Previously, he worked in investment banking at CIBC and Duff & Phelps.

William Jarvis, born in Dallas, Texas, graduated from the McDonough School of Business at Georgetown University in 2002. Upon graduation, he worked at GE Capital in its Financial Management Program and later at JPMorgan, as an analyst in the Leveraged Finance group of the investment bank, where he worked on numerous LBO and Restructuring transactions. William left JPMorgan to pursue his MBA at the Wharton School of the University of Pennsylvania.

Decrease your T/NJ Ratio
(Time to New Job)

Use the Internet's most targeted job search tools for finance professionals.

Vault Finance Job Board

The most comprehensive and convenient job board for finance professionals. Target your search by area of finance, function, and experience level, and find the job openings that you want. No surfing required.

VaultMatch Resume Database

Vault takes match-making to the next level: post your resume and customize your search by area of finance, experience and more. We'll match job listings with your interests and criteria and e-mail them directly to your inbox.

GO FOR THE GOLD!

**GET VAULT GOLD MEMBERSHIP
AND GET ACCESS TO ALL OF VAULT'S
AWARD-WINNING FINANCE CAREER INFORMATION**

◆ **Employee surveys** on 100s of top finance employers with insider info on:

  • Company culture
  • Salaries and compensation
  • Hiring process and interviews
  • Business outlook

◆ **Access to 100+ extended** insider finance employer profiles

◆ Complete access to **Vault's exclusive finance firm rankings**, including quality of life rankings

◆ Insider salary info with **Vault's Finance Salary Central**

◆ **Student and alumni surveys** for 100s of top MBA programs and law schools

◆ Receive Vault's **Finance Job Alerts** of top jobs posted on the Vault Finance Job Board

◆ Access to complete **Vault message board archives**

◆ **15% off** all Vault purchases, including Vault Guide and Finance Employer Profiles, Vault's Finance Interview Prep and Vault Resume Reviews (the WSJ's "top choice")

VᴧULT
> the most trusted name in career information